RENAL

DIET

COOKBOOK

Healthy Recipes With Low Sodium And Low Potassium Than Anyone Can Quickly Cook At Home. Manage Kidney Disease By Eating Tasty Dishes

Alexander Brown

TABLE OF CONTENTS

INTRODUCTION 9

ABOUT KIDNEY DISEASE........................11

THE 5 STAGES OF KIDNEY DISEASE 14

KIDNEY FAILURE POSSIBLE
TREATMENT 16

THE RENAL DIET..............................21

LISTS OF FOOD RECOMMENDED 24

LIST OF FOODS TO AVOID......................26

TIPS TO EAT ENOUGH CALORIES
WITHOUT GOING OVER LIMITS OF
HARMFUL NUTRIENTS (IN PARTICULAR
OVER PROTEIN) 28

BREAKFAST 31

1. Apple Pumpkin Muffins 31

2. Blueberry Citrus Muffins 31

3. Blueberry Bread Pudding 32

4. Old-Fashioned Pancakes 33

5. Tender Oatmeal Pancakes...................33

6. Spiced French Toast 34

7. Breakfast Tacos 34

8. Baked Egg Casserole 35

9. Bell Pepper and Feta Crustless Quiche 35

10. Egg White and Broccoli Omelet...................36

11. Yogurt Parfait with Strawberries 37

12. Mexican Scrambled Eggs in Tortilla 37

13. American Blueberry Pancakes.....................37

14. Raspberry Peach Breakfast Smoothie 38

15. Fast Microwave Egg Scramble.....................38

16. Mango Lassi Smoothie 39

17. Breakfast Maple Sausage 39

18. Summer Veggie Omelet 39

19. Raspberry Overnight Porridge.....................40

20. Cheesy Scrambled Eggs with Fresh Herbs.....40

21. Turkey and Spinach Scramble on Melba Toast 41

22. Vegetable Omelet 41

23. Breakfast Salad from Grains and Fruits 42

24. French Toast with Applesauce 42

LUNCH 44

25. Bagels Made Healthy 44

26. Cornbread with Southern Twist 44

27. Grandma's Pancake Special 45

28. Pasta with Indian Lentils 45

29. Mexican Style Burritos 46

30. Sweet Pancakes 46

31. Buckwheat and Grapefruit Porridge 46

32. Egg and Veggie Muffins 47

33. Cherry Berry Bulgur Bowl 47

34. Sausage Breakfast Casserole 48

35. Chicken Wild Rice Soup 48

36. Chicken Noodle Soup 49

37. Cucumber Soup 49

38. Squash and Turmeric Soup 50

39. Leek, Potato and Carrot Soup 50

40. Roasted Red Pepper Soup 51

41. Yucatan Soup 51

42. Zesty Taco Soup 52

43. Southwestern Posole 53

44. Wild Rice Asparagus Soup 53

45. Nutmeg Chicken Soup 54

46. Hungarian Cherry Soup 54

47. Italian Wedding Soup 55

48. Old Fashioned Salmon Soup 55

49. Oxtail Soup 56

50. Classic Chicken Soup 56

51. Beef Okra Soup 57

52. Green Bean Veggie Stew 57

53. Chicken Pasta Soup 58

54. Cabbage Turkey Soup 58

55. Chicken Fajita Soup 59

56. Cream of Chicken Soup 59

57. Beef Stroganoff Soup 60

58. Paprika Pork Soup 61

59. Green Chicken Enchilada Soup 61

60. Hawaiian Chicken Salad 62

61. Grated Carrot Salad with Lemon-Dijon Vinaigrette 62

62. Tuna Macaroni Salad 62

63. Couscous Salad 63

64. Fruity Zucchini Salad 63

65. Cucumber Salad, Pulled Through Slowly 63

66. Tortellini Salad 64

67. Farmer's Salad 64

68. Chicken and Asparagus Salad with Watercress 65

69. Cucumber Salad 65

70. Broccoli-Cauliflower Salad 66

71. Macaroni Salad 66

72. Pear & Brie Salad 66

73.	Creamy Tuna Salad	67
74.	Caesar Salad	67
75.	Thai Cucumber Salad	67
76.	Barb's Asian Slaw	68
77.	Green Bean and Potato Salad	68
78.	Italian Cucumber Salad	69
79.	Grapes Jicama Salad	69
80.	Cucumber Couscous Salad	69

DINNER 71

81.	Spring Vegetable Soup	71
82.	Seafood Corn Chowder	71
83.	Beef Sage Soup	72
84.	Cabbage Borscht	72
85.	Ground Beef Soup	73
86.	Shrimp and Crab Gumbo	73
87.	Tangy Turkey Soup	74
88.	Spaghetti Squash & Yellow Bell-Pepper Soup	75
89.	Red Pepper & Brie Soup	75
90.	Turkey & Lemon-Grass Soup	76
91.	Curried Fish Cakes	76
92.	Shrimp Fettuccine	77
93.	Baked Sole with Caramelized Onion	78
94.	Veggie Seafood Stir-Fry	79
95.	Thai Tuna Wraps	79
96.	Grilled Fish and Vegetable Packets	80
97.	Scrambled Eggs with Crab	80
98.	Grilled Cod	81
99.	Cod and Green Bean Curry	81
100.	White Fish Soup	82
101.	Lemon- Rosemary Cod Fillets	83
102.	Onion Dijon Crusted Catfish	83
103.	Herb Baked Tuna	84
104.	Cilantro Lime Salmon	84
105.	Asian Ginger tuna	85
106.	Cheesy Tuna Chowder	85
107.	Lemon Butter Salmon	86
108.	Tofu Stir Fry	87
109.	Broccoli Pancake	87
110.	Carrot Casserole	88
111.	Cauliflower Rice	88
112.	Eggplant Fries	89
113.	Seasoned Green Beans	89
114.	Grilled Squash	90
115.	Thai Tofu Broth	90
116.	Delicious Vegetarian Lasagna	90
117.	Chili Tofu Noodles	91
118.	Curried Cauliflower	92

119. Elegant Veggie Tortillas 92

120. Simple Broccoli Stir-Fry 93

121. Braised Cabbage 93

122. Salad with Strawberries and Goat Cheese 94

123. Roasted Veggies Mediterranean Style.......... 94

124. Fruity Garden Lettuce Salad 95

125. Baked Dilly Pickerel.......................... 95

126. Rice Salad..................................... 95

127. Baked Eggplant Tray........................... 96

128. Raw Vegetables. Chopped Salad 97

129. Roasted Citrus Chicken........................ 98

130. Chicken with Asian Vegetables 98

131. Chicken Adobo 99

132. Chicken and Veggie Soup 99

133. Turkey Sausages............................... 100

134. Rosemary Chicken.............................. 100

135. Smoky Turkey Chili............................ 101

136. Avocado-Orange Grilled Chicken............... 101

137. Herbs and Lemony Roasted Chicken 102

138. Ground Chicken & Peas Curry 102

139. Chicken Meatballs Curry 103

140. Ground Chicken with Basil 104

141. Chicken &Veggie Casserole 105

142. Chicken & Cauliflower Rice Casserole......... 105

143. Chicken Meatloaf with Veggies................. 106

144. Roasted Spatchcock Chicken.................... 107

145. Creamy Mushroom and Broccoli Chicken... 108

DESERTS 109

146. Dessert Cocktail 109

147. Baked Egg Custard 109

148. Apple Crunch Pie 110

149. Pound Cake with Pineapple 110

150. Gumdrop Cookies 111

151. Spiced Peaches 111

152. Pumpkin Cheesecake Bar 112

153. Blueberry Mini Muffins........................ 112

154. Vanilla Custard 113

155. Chocolate Chip Cookies 113

156. Lemon Mousse 113

157. Jalapeno Crisp................................ 114

158. Raspberry Popsicle 114

159. Easy Fudge................................... 115

160. Coconut Loaf.................................. 115

161. Chocolate Parfait 115

162. Cauliflower Bagel............................. 116

163. Almond Crackers............................... 116

164. Cashew and Almond Butter 117

165. Nut and Chia Mix.................................117

166. Hearty Cucumber Bites.......................117

167. Hearty Almond Bread.........................118

168. Medjool Balls 118

169. Blueberry Pudding..............................119

170. Chia Seed Pumpkin Pudding 119

171. Parsley Souffle 119

172. Crunchy Banana Cookies 120

173. Fluffy Mock Pancakes.........................120

174. Baked Zucchini Chips..........................121

175. Mixes of Snack 122

176. Parmesan Crisps 122

177. Crispy Tomato Chips...........................122

178. Easy Ham and Dill Pickle Bites 123

179. Tasty Salmon Sandwich......................124

180. Creamy Soft-Scrambled Eggs 124

181. Cranberry Dip with Fresh Fruit 125

182. Cucumbers with Sour Cream 125

183. Sweet Savory Meatballs 126

184. Spicy Corn Bread 126

185. Sweet and Spicy Tortilla Chips.............127

186. Addictive Pretzels..............................127

187. Shrimp Spread with Crackers 128

188. Buffalo Chicken Dip 128

189. Chicken Pepper Bacon Wraps 129

190. Garlic Oyster Crackers................................129

191. Lime Cilantro Rice 129

DRINKS.. 131

192. Berry Shake..131

193. Watermelon Sorbet 131

194. Berry Smoothie...131

195. Berry and Almond Smoothie.....................132

196. Mango and Pear Smoothie........................132

197. Pineapple Juice 132

198. Coffee Smoothie 133

199. Blackberry and Apple Smoothie.................133

200. Minty Cherry Smoothie.............................133

201. Fruit Smoothie 134

202. The Green Minty Smoothie 134

203. Mocha Milk Shake 134

204. Gut Cleansing Smoothie............................135

205. Cabbage and Chia Glass 135

206. Blueberry and Kale Mix............................135

207. Rosemary and Lemon Garden Smoothie 136

208. Melon and Coconut Dish...........................136

209. Blueberry Smoothie 136

210. Citrus Shake 137

211. **Cucumber and Lemon-Flavored Water**.......137

212. **Hot Mulled Punch** 137

30 DAYS MEAL PLAN.............................. 139

INDEX.. 142

CONCLUSION... 146

INTRODUCTION

Human health hangs in a complete balance when all of its interconnected bodily mechanisms function properly in perfect sync. Without its major organs working normally, the body soon suffers indelible damage. Kidney malfunction is one such example, and it is not just the entire water balance that is disturbed by the kidney disease, but a number of other diseases also emerge due to this problem. Kidney disorders are progressive in nature, which means that if they are not treated and managed properly, they might lead to permanent kidney damage. That is why it is critical to regulate and manage the condition and limit its progression, which can be accomplished using both medical and natural methods. While drugs can only guarantee a cure in thirty percent of cases, a change in lifestyle and food can be miraculous, with seventy percent of cures guaranteed. A kidney-friendly diet and lifestyle not only keeps extra minerals out of the kidneys but also helps drugs work more effectively. As a result, treatment without a healthy diet is ineffective. We'll cover the basics of kidney illness, including symptoms, causes, and diagnostics, in this renal diet cookbook. This preamble will help readers comprehend the situation more clearly; after that, we'll talk about the importance of a renal diet and a kidney-friendly lifestyle in preventing diseases. Not only that, but the book also includes a variety of delectable renal diet recipes that promise delectable flavors and good health.

Despite their tiny size, the kidneys perform a number of functions that are vital for the body to be able to function healthily.

These include:

· Creating the enzyme known as renin which regulates blood pressure,

· Ensuring bone marrow creates red blood cells,

· Controlling calcium and phosphorus levels through absorption and excretion.

Unfortunately, when kidney disease reaches a chronic stage, these functions start to stop working. However, with the right treatment and lifestyle, it is possible to manage symptoms and continue living well. This is even more applicable in the earlier stages of the disease. Tactlessly, 10% of all adults over the age of 20 will experience some form of kidney disease in their lifetime. There are a variety of different treatments for kidney disease, which depend on the cause of the disease.

Kidney (or renal) diseases are affecting around 14% of the adult population, according to international stats. In the US, approx. 661.000 Americans suffer from kidney dysfunction. Out of these patients, 468.000 proceed to dialysis treatment, and the rest have one active kidney transplant.

The high quantities of diabetes and heart illness are additionally related to kidney dysfunction, and sometimes one condition, for example diabetes, may prompt the other.

With such a significant number of high rates, possibly the best course of treatment is the contravention of dialysis, which makes people depend upon clinical and crisis facility meds on any occasion multiple times every week. In this manner, if your kidney has just given a few indications of brokenness, you can forestall dialysis through an eating routine, something that we will talk about in this book.

ABOUT KIDNEY DISEASE

T he words kidney function, and renal function is used to describe how well the kidneys work. Every healthy person is born with a pair of kidneys. Because of the other kidney's function, anytime one of the kidneys lost function, it went unreported. However, if the kidney functions continue to deteriorate and reach a level as low as 25%, the situation becomes dangerous for the patients. People with only one functioning kidney require competent external therapy and, in the worst-case scenario, a kidney transplant.

When a number of renal cells called nephrons are partially or totally destroyed, they fail to filter blood entering the body properly, resulting in kidney disease. The slow deterioration of kidney cells can be caused by a number of factors, including an acidic or toxic build-up inside the kidney over time, genetics, or other kidney-damaging disorders such as hypertension (high blood pressure) or diabetes.

Chronic Kidney Disease (CKD)

CKD or chronic kidney disease is the stage of kidney damage where it fails to filter the blood properly. The term chronic is used to refer to gradual and long-term damage to an organ. Therefore, chronic kidney disease is developed after a slow—yet progressive—damage to the kidneys. The symptoms of this disease only appear when the toxic wastes start to build up in the body. Therefore, such a stage should be prevented at all costs. Hence, early diagnosis of the disease proves to be significant. The sooner the patient realizes the gravity of the situation, the better measures they can take to curb the problem.

What about after we are affected by diseases? Well, even then, we make sure that we spend less time pondering about and trying to change what we cannot and more time on how to take care of ourselves. By focusing on our own actions, we gain more confidence, motivation, and knowledge. We realize that the ability to make changes, however big or small, lies within us.

In the case of chronic kidney diseases, we have the power to ensure that the disease does not get worse.

Causes of Kidney Disease

According to the National Kidney Foundation, the main 2 causes of chronic kidney disease are high blood pressure and diabetes. If you visit a doctor, health expert, or diet consultant, then you will realize that one of the major ways in managing your blood pressure and preventing diabetes is a healthy diet.

As the blood pressure or diabetes levels get worse, so does the amount of waste buildup. The waste goes into your blood faster than the kidneys are able to filter them. At this point, your kidneys are like an overworked employee at a firm; there is so much work still remaining but only a small amount of time to get finished during a particular period. The kidneys begin to deteriorate over time. The filters begin to leak, unable to hold on to the waste buildup anymore. Only a small percentage of the entire waste gets filtered properly, with the rest entering the bloodstream. For some, the time it takes for kidney failure might be months, while for others, the kidneys could worsen across a span of years. It all depends on numerous factors like diet, lifestyle choices, and even genetics.

Pretty soon, you might feel like your kidney functions have been kidnapped; they don't seem to be functioning well anymore, or they barely exist. But that is not the case. Think of the example of the overworked employee that we used earlier. At some point, the employee could collapse out of dehydration or exhaustion. In a similar way, kidney disease causes the organs to fail, which causes numerous problems such as low energy, high exhaustion levels, sleep difficulties, poor appetite, swollen ankles and feet, and the need to urinate more often, especially at night.

Understanding the Symptoms

The good thing is that we can prevent the chronic stage of renal disease by identifying the early signs of any form of kidney damage. Even when a person feels minor changes in their body, they should consult an expert to confirm if it might lead to something serious. The following are a few of the early symptoms of renal damage:

Tiredness or drowsiness

Muscle cramps

Loss of appetite

Changes in the frequency of urination

Swelling of hands and feet

A feeling of itchiness

Numbness

The darkness of skin

Trouble in sleeping

Shortness of breath

The feeling of nausea or vomiting

These symptoms can appear in combination with one another. These are general signs of body malfunction, and they should never be ignored. And if they are left unnoticed, they can lead to worsening of the condition and may appear as:

Back pain

Abdominal pain

Fever

Rash

Diarrhea

Nosebleeds

Vomiting

After witnessing any of these symptoms, a person should immediately consult a health expert and prepare themself for the required lifestyle changes.

THE 5 STAGES OF KIDNEY DISEASE

Chronic kidney disease is categorized into 5 stages, each one characterized by a certain degree of damage done to the kidneys and the rate of glomerular filtration, which is the rate at which filtration takes place in the kidneys. These help us understand just how well the kidneys are functioning.

Stage 1

The first stage is the least severe and actually comes close to a healthy state of your kidneys. Most people will never be aware if they have entered stage 1 of chronic kidney disease or CKD. In many cases, if people discover stage 1 CKD, then it is because they were being tested for diabetes or high blood pressure. Otherwise, people can find out about stage 1 CKD if they discover protein or blood in the urine, signs of kidney damage in an ultrasound, a computerized tomography (CT) scan, or through magnetic resonance imaging (MRI). If people have a family history of polycystic kidney disease (PKD), then there are chances that they might have CKD as well.

Stage 2

In this stage, there is a mild decrease in the glomerular filtration rate. People don't usually notice any symptoms at this stage as well. The reasons for discovering any signs of CKD are the same as with the reasons provided in stage 1.

So, what's the difference between stage 1 and stage 2? It all lies in the glomerular filtration rate, or GFR for short. The GFR is measured in milliliters/minute.

In stage 1, the glomerular filtration rate (GFR) is around 90 ml./minutes. The normal range of the GFR is from 90–120 ml./minutes. So, as you can see, stage 1 CKD shows a GFR at the lower end of the range. Because it falls so close to a normal rate, it easily goes unnoticed. At stage 2, the GFR falls to between 60–89 ml./minutes. You might become concerned with the range stage 2 falls in, but your kidneys are actually resilient. Even if they are not functioning at 100%, your kidneys are capable of doing a good job. So good that you might not notice anything was out of the ordinary.

Even though the differences between stages 1 and 2 are minuscule, they cannot be combined because the chances of someone showing certain symptoms of CKD when in stage 2 are greater.

Stage 3

At this stage, the kidneys suffer moderate damage. In order to properly gauge the level of damage, this stage is further divided into 2: stage 3A and stage 3B. The reason for the division is that even though the severity of the disease worsens from 3A to 3B, the damage to the kidneys is still within moderate levels.

Each of the divisions is characterized by their GFR:

3A has a GFR between 45–59 ml/minute.

3B has a GFR between 30–44 ml/minute.

When patients reach stage 3, they begin to experience other symptoms of CKD, which include the following:

Increase in fatigue

Shortness of breath and swelling of extremities—also called edema

Slight kidney pain, where the pain is felt in the lower back area

Change in the color of urine

Stage 4

At stage 4, the kidney disease becomes severe. The GFR falls down to 15–30 ml/minutes. As the waste buildup increases, the patient might experience nausea and vomiting, a buildup of urea in the blood that could cause bad breath, and find themselves having trouble doing everyday tasks such as reading a newspaper or trying to write up an email.

It is important to see a nephrologist (a doctor who specializes in kidney problems) when the patient reaches stage 4.

Stage 5

At stage 5, the kidneys have a GFR of less than 15 ml./minutes. This is a truly low rate that causes the waste buildup to reach a critical point. The organs have reached an advanced stage of CKD, causing them to lose almost all their abilities in order to function normally.

KIDNEY FAILURE POSSIBLE TREATMENT

I f you experience kidney failure, then you have 2 options: You can look for a donor who might be able to donate one of their kidneys or you may want to opt for dialysis.

Dialysis is an expensive and recurring process that you will need to do over and over again, depending on the condition of your kidneys.

Transplant, on the other hand, is mostly a one-time major expense, given that you are able to find a perfect match.

But regardless of the path you decide to choose, there are thousands of people who have led a healthy and normal life, even with dialysis/kidney transplants. So, even if you are a victim, don't lose all your hopes just yet.

Let me talk a little bit about dialysis.

Dialysis

Dialysis is basically a process that helps to get rid of toxins and extra fluid buildup in your body through artificial means. However, an external machine won't really be able to do everything that your kidney can do, so even with dialysis, you might face some complications in the long run. However, there are 2 types of dialysis:

Peritoneal Dialysis

This form of treatment tries to cleanse your blood by utilizing the lining of your abdominal area and a cleansing solution known as Dialysate. The best part about this dialysis is that it can easily be done at home, as long as you have a clean and private area.

Hemodialysis

This particular treatment is also known as Hemo and is the most common one for kidney failures. This form of dialysis utilizes a machine to filter and clean out your blood. It is also recommended that you do this at a hospital; however, if you have the budget, then it is possible to do it at home, as well.

After dialysis is the kidney transplant.

Kidney Transplant

A kidney transplant, as the name implies, is essentially a surgery that gives you a healthy kidney from a donor's body. It is possible to have a kidney donated from a live body or a donor who has already died but has donated their kidney for a good cause. As mentioned above, if you can get a healthy kidney, then it is possible to lead a completely normal life.

And lastly, you can try medical management.

Medical Management

If you have budget issues or just want to avoid dialysis or transplant altogether, then there are some medical solutions that you might look into to reduce the symptoms of kidney failure.

They won't completely reverse the effects, but they might let you stay healthy until your kidneys are unable to function anymore.

If you opt for medical management, then the first thing to do is consult with your physician, as they will be able to point you in the right direction.

They will create a care plan for you that will guide you on what you should do and what you should not do. Ensure you always keep a copy of the plan wherever you go and discuss the terms with your loved ones as well.

It should also be noted that most individuals who tend to go for medical management opt for hospice care.

The real aim of hospice care is to try and decrease your pain and improve the quality of your final days before you die.

In medical management, you can expect a hospice to:

Help you by providing you with a nursing home

Help your family and friends to support you

Try to improve the quality of your life as much as possible

Try to provide medications and care to help you manage your symptoms

But always have it in mind that regardless of which path you take, always discuss everything with your doctor.

Learning to Deal with Kidney Failure

Learning that you are suffering from kidney failure might be a difficult thing to cope with. No matter how long you have been preparing for the inevitable, this is something that will come as a shock to you.

But, as mentioned earlier, just because you have started dialysis doesn't mean that everything that you hold dear has to come to an end!

It might be a little bit difficult at first to get yourself oriented to a new routine, but once you are into the groove, you'll start feeling much better.

Your nurses, loved ones, doctors, and co-workers will all be there to support you.

To make things easier, though, let me break down the individual types of problems that you might face and how you can deal with them:

Stress During Kidney Failure

When you are suffering from kidney failure, it's normal to be stressed out all the time. This might lead you to skip meals or even to forget your medication, which might affect your health even more.

But you need to understand that life is full of hurdles and setbacks, and you really can't let them hold you back.

In that light, here are 6 tips to help you keep your stress under control:

Make sure to take some time to just relax and unwind. Try to practice deep breathing, visualization, meditation, or even muscle relaxation. All of these will help you to stay calm and keep your body healthy.

Make sure to involve yourself in regular exercise. Take a hike, ride a bicycle or just simply take a jog. They all help. And if those aren't your thing, then you can always go for something more soothing, like tai chi or yoga.

When you are feeling too stressed, try to call up a friend or a beloved family member and talk to them. And if that's not helping, you can always take help from a psychiatrist/counselor.

Try to accept the things that are not under your control, and you can't change. Trying to enforce a change on something that is not within your reach will only make things worse for you. Better advice is to look for better ways of handling the situation instead of trying to change it.

Don't put too much pressure on yourself; try to be good to yourself and don't expect much. You are a human being after all, right? You can make mistakes, so accept that. Just try your best.

And lastly, always try to maintain a positive attitude. Even when things go completely wrong, try to see the good instead of the bad and focus on that. Try to find things in all phases of your life that make you happy and that you appreciate, such as your friends, work, health, and family, for example. You have no idea how much help a simple change of perspective can bring.

And on the topic of working out...

Exercise

Apart from the special diet, such as the renal diet, physical activity is another way through which you can improve the quality of your life.

This might be a little bit tough to do if you are alone, but it is very much possible. However, you should have in mind that working out alone won't help you; you must work out and follow a well-balanced, healthy diet.

Both of these combined will go to great lengths to help you lose weight and control your disease.

In fact, a study has shown that people who try to complete 10,1000 steps per day and work out for about 2 ½ hours every week while cutting down 500–800 calories per day and following a proper diet routinely have a 50% chance of reducing blood sugar to normal levels, which will further help you to stay healthy.

Common forms of exercise include:

Stair climbing

Tai chi

Stretching

Yoga

Cycling

Walking

Swimming

To perform these normal workouts, you don't have to join a gym or even buy any sort of expensive equipment! You can simply take a walk around your streets, do yoga at home, and so on.

Just make sure to consult with your doctor to find out which exercises are suitable for you and adjust them to your dialysis routine.

Anxiety and Depression

These 2 are possibly the most prominent issues that you are going to face. A feeling of depression might last for a long period of time if left unattended. Anxiety might come at the same time, but it won't last for long.

Either way, mood swings will occur that will suddenly make you sad.

However, you should know that it is completely normal to feel anxious or sad when you're going through such a huge change in life. This is even more prominent if you start taking dialysis, as it will require you to completely change your daily routine and follow a different type of diet.

During this adjusting phase, you'll feel many emotions, such as anger, fear, sadness, etc.

To summarize, the symptoms of depression are:

Loss of interest

Loss of any appetite

Sleeping problems

On the other hand, symptoms of anxiety are:

Constant sweating

Quick breathing

Inconsistent heartbeat

Constant troubling thoughts

Regardless, the main thing to know is that you are not alone in this fight. Thousands of people have and are going through the same experience. Many people often feel left alone and lose the will to fight, but it doesn't have to be the same for you.

Help is always available! Try sharing with your family members, join support groups, talk to a social worker, etc.

It doesn't matter what your situation is; if you just reach out to the right person, then you will always find the help and support that you need.

THE RENAL DIET

The Benefits of Renal diet

If you have kidney dysfunction, a proper diet is necessary for controlling the amount of toxic waste in the bloodstream. When toxic waste piles up in the system along with increased fluid, chronic inflammation occurs and we have a much higher chance of developing cardiovascular, bone, metabolic or other health issues.

Since your kidneys can't fully get rid of the waste on their own, which comes from food and drinks, probably the only natural way to help our system is through this diet.

A renal diet is especially useful during the first stages of kidney dysfunction and leads to the following benefits:

● Prevents excess fluid and waste build-up

● prevents the progression of renal dysfunction stages

● Decreases the likelihood of developing other chronic health problems e.g. heart disorders

● has a mild antioxidant function in the body, which keeps inflammation and inflammatory responses under control.

The above-mentioned benefits are noticeable once the patient follows the diet for at least a month and then continuing it for longer periods, to avoid the stage where dialysis is needed. The strictness of the diet depends on the current stage of renal/kidney disease, if, for example, you are in the 3rd or 4th stage, you should follow a stricter diet and be attentive to the food, which is allowed or prohibited.

Nutrients You Need

Potassium

Potassium occurs naturally in nearly all foods, in varying amounts. Our bodies need an amount of potassium to help with muscle activity as well as electrolyte balance and regulation of blood pressure. However, if potassium is in excess within the system and the kidneys can't expel it (due to renal disease), fluid retention and muscle spasms can occur.

Phosphorus

Phosphorus is a trace mineral found in a wide range of foods and especially dairy, meat, and eggs. It acts synergistic ally with calcium as well as Vitamin D to promote bone health. However, when there is damage to the kidneys, excess amounts of the mineral cannot be taken out and this can cause bone weakness.

Calories

When being on a renal diet, it is vital to give yourself the right number of calories to fuel your system. The exact number of calories you should consume daily depends on your age, gender, general health status and stage of renal disease. In most cases though, there are no strict limitations in the calorie intake, as long as you take them from proper sources that are low in sodium, potassium, and phosphorus. In general, doctors recommend a daily limit between 1800-2100 calories per day to keep weight within the normal range.

Protein

Protein is an essential nutrient that our systems need to develop and generate new connective tissue e.g. muscles, even during injuries. Protein also helps stop bleeding and supports the immune system in fighting infections. A healthy adult with no kidney disease would usually need 40-65 grams of protein per day.

However, in renal diet, protein consumption is a tricky subject as too much or too little can cause problems. Protein, when being metabolized by our systems also creates waste which is typically processed by the kidneys. But when kidneys are damaged or underperforming, as in the case of kidney disease that waste will stay in the system. This is why patients in more advanced CKD stages are advised to limit their protein consumption as well.

Fats

Our systems need fats and particularly good fats as a fuel source and for other metabolic cell functions. A diet rich in bad and Trans or saturated fats though can significantly raise the odds of developing heart problems, which often occur with renal disease. This is why most physicians advise their renal patients to follow a diet that contains a decent amount of good fats and a meager amount of Trans (processed) or saturated fat.

Sodium

Sodium is what our bodies need to regulate fluid and electrolyte balance. It also plays a role in normal cell division in the muscles and nervous system. However, in kidney disease, sodium can quickly spike at higher than normal levels and the kidneys will be unable to expel it causing fluid accumulation as a side-effect. Those who also suffer from heart problems as well should limit their consumption as it may raise blood pressure.

Carbohydrates

Carbs act as a major and quick fuel source for the body's cells. When we consume carbs, our systems turn them into glucose and then into energy for "feeding" our body cells. Carbs are generally not restricted in the renal diet. Still, some types of carbs contain dietary fiber as well, which helps regulate normal colon function and protect blood vessels from damage.

Dietary Fiber

Fiber is an important element in our system that cannot be properly digested but plays a key role in the regulation of our bowel movements and blood cell protection. The fiber in the renal diet is generally encouraged as it helps loosen up the stools, relieve constipation and bloating and protect from colon damage. However, many patients don't get enough amounts of dietary fiber per day as many of them are high in potassium or phosphorus. Fortunately, there are some good dietary fiber sources for CKD patients that have lower amounts of these minerals compared to others.

Vitamins/Minerals

Our systems, according to medical research, need at least 13 vitamins and minerals to keep our cells fully active and healthy. Patients with renal disease though are more likely to be depleted by water-soluble vitamins like B-complex and Vitamin C, as a result, or limited fluid consumption. Therefore, supplementation with these vitamins along with a renal diet program should help cover any possible vitamin deficiencies. Supplementation of fat-soluble vitamins like vitamins A, K, and E may be avoided as they can quickly build up in the system and turn toxic.

Fluids

When you are in an advanced stage of renal disease, fluid can quickly build-up and lead to problems. While it is important to keep your system well hydrated, you should avoid minerals like potassium and sodium which can trigger further fluid build-up and cause a host of other symptoms.

Nutrient You Need to Avoid

Salt or sodium is known for being one of the most important **ingredients** that the renal diet prohibits its use. This ingredient, although simple, can badly and strongly affect your body and especially the kidneys. Any excess sodium can't be easily filtered because of the failing condition of the kidneys. A large build-up of sodium can cause catastrophic results on your body. Potassium and Phosphorus are also prohibited for kidney patients depending on the stage of kidney disease.

LISTS OF FOOD RECOMMENDED

#1 Potatoes are an excellent source of potassium, which helps to regulate blood pressure and is essential in overall cardiovascular health. Potassium also helps the kidneys eliminate waste products from the body, including excess fluid that can build up in people with chronic kidney disease. Plant-based sources of protein will help boost nitrogen balance and may reduce inflammation. Protein is necessary for maintaining muscle mass during dialysis or transplantation, which can result in weight reduction, reduced appetite, stronger bones, and improved physical function both before and after the procedure.

#2 Beans (General) Beans are also an excellent source of potassium. Beans can be found in many different flavors, sizes, shapes and colors; cooked beans make a filling meal while dried beans can be rehydrated for cold salads.

#3 Lentils (General) Lentils are another good source of potassium. Before cooking, most dried beans must be soaked overnight, but lentils just need to soak for around an hour. Lentils can be eaten cooked or canned without being drained, unlike other beans that must be drained and rinsed before use. Canned lentils do not need to be rinsed prior to use; just check the label for sodium content.

#4 Vegetables (General) Vegetables are an excellent source of potassium; many vegetables are also packed with vitamins and minerals. Many vegetables are good sources of fiber, which can help normalize bowel movements in people with chronic kidney disease.

#5 Sweet Potatoes Sweet potatoes have a specific fiber called "beta-glucan" that is beneficial for people with chronic kidney disease. Beta-glucan helps lower the level of glucose in the blood, helping to reduce risks associated with diabetes. Sweet potatoes also contain a lot of vitamin A, which helps maintain good vision and may help protect eyes from the damage that occurs from some medications taken by people on dialysis or after a transplant. Vitamin A is also important for bone health, especially in children with chronic kidney disease. Sweet potatoes are easy to work into your diet because they can be baked, boiled, microwaved or prepared in a variety of different recipes.

#6 Peas (General) Peas are the small green vegetables that you find in cans mixed with cream cheese or as a side salad. Potassium and vitamin K are both abundant in them. Vitamin K is essential for bone health, particularly during dialysis or following a transplant.

#7 Kiwi Fruit Kiwi fruit contains vitamin C as well as fiber and potassium. Vitamin C helps the body absorb fat-soluble nutrients such as vitamin E and fatty acids. It may also play a role in lowering blood pressure and reducing risk of infection to the kidneys.

#8 Black Beans Black beans are also considered a good source of potassium and fiber, which helps to maintain bowel movements in people with chronic kidney disease. Black beans may be high in saturated fat, but they are still considered a nutritious choice for people with chronic kidney disease because they provide heart-healthy fats and protein.

#9 Green Peas (General) Green peas contain fiber and potassium and can be used in many different dish's recipes. Green peas look similar to fava beans, but with a different taste. They are sometimes preferred in salads because the green color helps the salads to appear more appetizing than when they do not have any color.

#10 White Beans White beans are another good source of potassium and fiber, which is important for bowel movement in people with chronic kidney disease. Beans can be found canned or dried. Canned beans may need to be rinsed prior to use; just check the label for sodium content.

#11 Pumpkin Seeds Pumpkin seeds contain protein, vitamin B1 (thiamin), vitamin E and magnesium, all of which help maintain a healthy heart and reduce risk factors associated with heart disease and high blood pressure.

#12 Kale is a green, leafy vegetable that is an excellent vitamin C and beta-carotene source. One cup of raw kale contains 4 milligrams of potassium. Kale can be used in salads, stir-fries, soups and even as pizza toppings.

#13 Eggs (General) Eggs are high in protein and vitamins such as A, D, and B12, which are essential for heart health and lowering risk factors for heart disease and high blood pressure.

They're also high in choline and lutein, two nutrients that may aid prevent artery hardening (or thickening).

#14 Poultry (General) Poultry is a good source of protein and vitamins such as A, D and B12, which are important for maintaining a healthy heart and reducing risk factors associated with heart disease and high blood pressure. It's also high in choline and lutein, two nutrients that may aid prevent artery hardening (or thickening).

#15 Dairy Foods [specifically [low fat [milk [with [fortified [calcium] [dairy products]. Milk with fortified calcium is essential for people with chronic kidney disease because it helps maintain bone density. Milk with fortified calcium is also fortified with vitamin D, which helps maintain bone density and may reduce the risk of brittle bones.

LIST OF FOODS TO AVOID

Potassium is an essential element for humans. Potassium is involved in many biochemical processes in the body, including cell membrane potential, muscle contraction, and nerve impulse transmission. A high intake of potassium-rich foods can help to prevent conditions such as heart disease, stroke, osteoporosis and hypertension. High potassium levels in the blood may increase the risk of kidney stones and lead to the depletion of other minerals like calcium and magnesium.

However, while a healthy diet with plenty of fruits and vegetables provides adequate amounts of potassium to combat these conditions without any negative side effects, it's also important to reduce intake if you're experiencing symptoms such as muscle weakness or numbness related to hypokalemia (low levels of potassium). If you have renal difficulties, talk to your doctor about how to control your dietary intake before reading the list of high potassium foods to avoid.

1. Molasses. Molasses is a byproduct of the sugar cane or sugar beet processing industry and is used to manufacture table sugar. It is rich in potassium, with an average level of 940 mg/10 g serving size. However, since it also contains a significant number of natural sugars and carbohydrates, which are believed to promote cardiovascular disease if consumed in excess, molasses is one of the foods that are high in potassium that you should limit or completely eliminate from your diet?

2. Soy sauce. You can find soy sauce, made from fermented soybeans and salt, in most Asian restaurants and grocery stores. It has a strong salty flavor combined with a sweet aftertaste and just one tablespoon (13 g) contains 541 mg of potassium. Soy sauce is also high in sodium and sodium chloride, which can cause bloating and hypertension over time. If you love the flavor of soy sauce, consider using it sparingly or limiting its use to once or twice a month at the table as part of home cooking rather than relying on it as a condiment for takeout foods such as dumplings or noodles.

3. Spinach. Spinach is high in magnesium, folate, calcium, and potassium, and is sometimes referred to as a "superfood." While it's true that eating lots of spinach will make you feel full longer without adding excess calories or sugar, the high fiber content of this dark leafy green vegetable can interfere with absorption of some nutrients when consumed with other foods. For example, if you eat spinach on top of a plate with rice or pasta when it's time to eat, your body may miss out on key nutrients such as potassium and vitamin K.

4. Avocados. Avocado is one of the highest sources of potassium among all fruits and vegetables (even more than bananas!). Just one medium-sized avocado, weighing approximately 225 g contains 845 mg of potassium. This is why it's important to keep the serving size in mind when you're deciding whether or not to eat avocados. One-fifth (1/5) of an avocado (100 g) is the average serving size used for most **nutrition**al analyses, but two-fifths (2/5) of an avocado is not uncommon at all for anyone who is trying to manage diet with avocado as one of the high potassium foods.

5. Ketchup. While ketchup is a popular condiment that is rich in sugar and salt, the tomato sauce that goes into it typically has a low sodium content. However, even lower sodium ketchup does have a significant amount of potassium as well as other nutrients such as calcium and vitamin C. Just one tablespoon (15 g) of ketchup contains 409 mg of potassium. If you're not accustomed to adding high potassium foods to your diet, consider limiting its use to once or twice a month at the table rather than using it as a condiment for all your favorite foods.

TIPS TO EAT ENOUGH CALORIES WITHOUT GOING OVER LIMITS OF HARMFUL NUTRIENTS (IN PARTICULAR OVER PROTEIN)

We have already made an emphasis on how important it is to cut your protein portions when on a renal diet while also managing to ingest enough protein so you wouldn't have further health complications.

Since you should be monitoring your protein intake carefully so you would be able to improve your overall health, we have compiled a quick checklist of things you need to look out for to keep your protein intake under control and at normal levels that won't put additional pressure on your vital organs.

Protein Control Check List

- Avoid processed meat such as sausage, salami, canned meat, and other meat products that may contain higher concentrations of sodium and potassium.
- Try having protein in the form of meat and fish only once a day. You may choose lunch or dinner as your meat/fish meal.
- Avoid adding salt to your meat—instead, use garlic powder, herbs, and different safe seasonings that we have listed in our Ultimate Renal Grocery List.
- Try baking, broiling, grilling, or steam cooking your meat instead of eating fried meat.
- Choose lean and fresh meat for improved health.
- Cut your protein portions.

Protein in Renal Diet.

The renal diet promotes healthy living with low and damaged renal function, different stages of chronic kidneys disorders, and has the ultimate goal to help improve renal health, as well as helping prevention of chronic kidneys issue in patients with high-risk rates.

Protein is an essential nutrient that our body needs for a variety of vital roles in our organism, among which is the overall ability of tissue repair as well as "feeding" our muscle mass. Especially when some of the body functions are weak, patients may need extra protein to be able to recover and improve their health; however, since kidneys have the role of processing protein.

Renal-Friendly Protein Sources.

As mentioned before, a renal diet does prescribe lower doses of protein and smaller portions of meat for chronic kidney disorders patients, but it does not recommend a complete absence of protein in your diet. Besides meat, there are plenty of protein sources that can be described as moderately friendly or completely renal diet-friendly and in compliance with the dietary requirements, while it is very important to have your daily dose of protein. As mentioned earlier in the book, the recommended dose of protein for renal patients is set at 0.8 mg per Kg of body weight and around 1.3 mg of protein per Kg of body weight, unless recommended otherwise by your physician.

We also mentioned protein called albumin, commonly found in our blood with the task of repairing tissue and maintaining tissue growth, which is why you shouldn't miss out on adding protein to your diet even though you need to cut down on meat portions. To keep up healthy levels of albumin and prevent further damage to your kidneys, we are recommending some top renal-friendly foods that should help you get your daily dose of protein without jeopardizing your health.

Chicken

Chicken may have extra potassium that you don't need when your renal functions are not performing well, which is why it is recommended to lower your consumption of protein. However, lean chicken meat, especially chicken breasts, is especially rich in protein and has a low concentration of fat, which is exactly what you want in your protein source. Avoid consuming chicken-based products in the form of pre-made chicken roast found in stores, as well as processed and canned meat, which is packed with potassium and sodium that you are looking to lower in your diet. One portion of chicken meat may contain up to 28 gr of protein.

Cheese

Cottage cheese might have the right amount of animal-based protein that your body needs, however, cottage cheese might have higher concentrations of sodium while it also has high levels of potassium. Try going for low-sodium cheese when looking for more protein sources other than meat. You should also note that low-sodium products such as cheese with lowered levels of this mineral, may offer increased potassium concentrations which you want to avoid unless specifically recommended by your doctor.

Eggs

You can have an egg substitute with low sodium and low potassium concentrations, but you can also eat eggs as long as you don't exaggerate in quantity. The best source of clean protein for you is found in egg whites, providing you with around 7 gr of protein.

Yogurt

When substituting meat, try having Greek yogurt instead, as this dairy product is less harmful to your rental system when compared to the effects milk can leave on your health when having problems with renal functions. One serving of Greek yogurt will provide you with approximately 20 gr of animal-based protein.

Tofu burgers

Tofu burgers and other tofu products may be a good alternative for protein sources where eating meat is not an option for a specific reason, while a serving of tofu will provide you the same amount of protein as egg whites from one egg.

Protein shake

Protein supplements that are compliant with the renal diet and approved by your physician may represent. Protein supplements can be mixed with fruit and drinks, as well as be added to your food, which can be a great way of adding protein where there are no options for eating meat or finding protein in other food sources.

Fish

You can get up to 20 gr of protein in one serving of fish such as salmon, which actually has lower concentrations of potassium when compared to other fish.

"Leftovers", too much protein might become a problem for patients with damaged kidneys. Since kidneys are unable to remove all the waste that remains from processing protein, the body becomes overwhelmed with toxic waste that can't leave the body. That is actually the main reason why renal diet prescribes and recommends smaller portions of protein for renal patients and people with a high risk of getting chronic kidney issues. Of course, the relationship between renal diet and protein is complimentary, as this dietary regimen still recommends not skipping on your protein meals even in case you don't eat meat. Protein intake in renal patients is especially recommended for people who had a successful kidney transplant surgery and are in the phase of recovery where protein is of vital significance.

Based on your test results discuss with your doctor how much protein you are allowed to have daily for more specific dietary requirements.

BREKFAST

1. Apple Pumpkin Muffins

Preparation Time: 15 minutes
Cooking Time: 20 minutes
Servings: 12
Difficulty: Easy

INGREDIENTS

- 1 cup all-purpose flour
- 1 cup wheat bran
- 2 teaspoons Phosphorus Powder
- 1 cup pumpkin purée
- ¼ cup honey
- ¼ cup olive oil
- 1 egg
- 1 teaspoon vanilla extract
- ½ cup cored diced apple

DIRECTIONS

1. Preheat the oven to 400°F.
2. Line 12 muffin cups with paper liners.
3. In a medium bowl, stir together the flour, wheat bran, and baking powder.
4. In a small bowl, whisk together the pumpkin, honey, olive oil, egg, and vanilla.
5. Stir the pumpkin mixture into the flour mixture until just combined.
6. Stir in the diced apple.
7. Spoon the batter into the prepared muffin cups.
8. Bake for about 20 minutes, or until a toothpick inserted in the center of a muffin comes out clean.

NUTRITION PER SERVING: (1 muffin): Calories: 125; Total Fat: 5g; Saturated Fat: 1g; Cholesterol: 18mg; Sodium: 8mg; Carbohydrates: 20g; Fiber: 3g; Phosphorus: 120mg; Potassium: 177mg; Protein: 2g

2. Blueberry Citrus Muffins

Preparation Time: 15 minutes
Cooking Time: 25 minutes
Servings: 12
Difficulty: Easy

INGREDIENTS

- ½ cup coconut oil, melted
- 1 cup sugar
- 2 eggs

- 1 cup Homemade Rice Milk (or use unsweetened store-bought)
- ½ cup light sour cream
- 2 cups all-purpose flour
- 1 teaspoon freshly grated lemon zest
- 1 teaspoon freshly grated lime zest
- 2 teaspoons Phosphorus-Free Baking Powder
- 2 cups fresh blueberries

DIRECTIONS

1. Preheat the oven to 400°F.
2. Line 12 muffin cups with paper liners.
3. In a medium bowl, beat together the coconut oil and sugar with a hand mixer until very fluffy. Then beat in the eggs, rice milk, and sour cream until well blended, scraping down the sides of the bowl.
4. In a small bowl, stir together the flour, lemon zest, lime zest, and baking powder.
5. Stir the flour mixture into the egg mixture until just combined.
6. Stir in the blueberries.
7. Spoon the batter into the prepared muffin cups.
8. Bake about 25 minutes, or until a toothpick inserted in the center of a muffin comes out clean.

NUTRITION PER SERVING: (1 muffin): Calories: 252; Total fat: 9g; Saturated fat: 8g; Cholesterol: 36mg; Sodium: 26mg; Carbohydrates: 38g; Fiber: 1g; Phosphorus: 79mg; Potassium: 107mg; Protein: 4g

3. Blueberry Bread Pudding

Preparation Time: 10 minutes (plus 30 minutes soaking time)
Cooking Time: 35 minutes
Servings: 6
Difficulty: medium
INGREDIENTS

- 3 cups Homemade Rice Milk (or use unsweetened store-bought)
- ½ cup honey
- 3 eggs
- 2 teaspoons vanilla extract
- ½ teaspoon ground cinnamon
- 6 cups sourdough bread cubes
- 2 cups fresh blueberries

DIRECTIONS

1. Preheat the oven to 350°F.
2. In a large bowl, whisk together the rice milk, honey, eggs, vanilla, and cinnamon until well blended.
3. Stir in the bread cubes, and let the mixture soak for 30 minutes.
4. Stir in the blueberries. Spoon the mixture into a 9-by-13-inch baking dish.
5. Bake about 35 minutes, or until a knife inserted in the center comes out clean.
6. Low-sodium tip Sourdough bread has a delicious tangy flavor but is high in sodium, about 208 mg per

slice. Change this ingredient to a low-sodium white bread, and you'll cut the sodium per serving to 156mg.

NUTRITION PER SERVING: Calories: 382; Total fat: 4g; Saturated fat: 1g; Cholesterol: 106mg; Sodium: 378mg; Carbohydrates: 67g; Fiber: 3g; Phosphorus: 120mg; Potassium: 170mg; Protein: 11g

4. Old-Fashioned Pancakes

Preparation Time: 15 minutes
Cooking Time: 12 minutes
Servings: 4
Difficulty: Easy
INGREDIENTS
- 1 cup all-purpose flour
- ½ cup sugar
- ½ teaspoon Phosphorus-Free Baking Powder
- 1 cup Homemade Rice Milk (or use unsweetened store-bought)
- 2 eggs
- 1 tablespoon unsalted butter, divided

DIRECTIONS
1. In a medium bowl, stir together the flour, sugar, and baking powder.
2. In a small bowl, whisk together the rice milk and eggs.
3. Add the milk mixture to the flour mixture, and whisk until combined.
4. In a large skillet over medium heat, melt half the butter.
5. Scoop the batter, about ¼ cup for each pancake, into the skillet, and cook the pancakes until the edges are firm and the bottoms are golden, about 3 minutes.
6. Flip the pancakes and cook until golden brown, about 2 minutes.
7. Repeat with the remaining butter and batter.
8. Serve the pancakes hot.

NUTRITION PER SERVING: Calories: 272; Total fat: 6g; Saturated fat: 3g; Cholesterol: 113mg; Sodium: 20mg; Carbohydrates: 49g; Fiber: 1g; Phosphorus: 120mg; Potassium: 131mg; Protein: 6g

5. Tender Oatmeal Pancakes

Preparation Time: 15 minutes
Cooking Time: 12 minutes
Servings: 4
Difficulty: Easy
INGREDIENTS
- 1 cup all-purpose flour
- ¼ cup rolled oats
- Pinch ground cinnamon
- ½ cup Homemade Rice Milk (or use unsweetened store-bought)
- 1 large egg
- 1 tablespoon unsalted butter, divided

DIRECTIONS
1. In a medium bowl, stir together the flour, oats, and cinnamon.
2. In a small bowl, whisk together the rice milk and egg.
3. Add the rice milk mixture to the flour mixture, and whisk to combine well.
4. Place a large skillet over medium heat, and melt half the butter.

5. Scoop the batter, about ¼ cup for each pancake, into the skillet, and cook the pancakes until the edges are firm and the bottoms are golden, about 3 minutes.

6. Flip the pancakes and cook until golden brown, about 2 minutes.

7. Repeat with the remaining butter and batter.

8. Serve the pancakes hot.

NUTRITION PER SERVING: Calories: 195; Total fat: 5g; Saturated fat: 2g; Cholesterol: 60mg; Sodium: 19mg; Carbohydrates: 30g; Fiber: 2g; Phosphorus: 109mg; Potassium: 92mg; Protein: 6g

6. Spiced French Toast

Preparation Time: 15 minutes
Cooking Time: 12 minutes
Servings: 4
Difficulty: Easy
INGREDIENTS
- 4 eggs
- ½ cup Homemade Rice Milk (here, or use unsweetened store-bought) or almond milk
- ¼ cup freshly squeezed orange juice
- 1 teaspoon ground cinnamon
- ½ teaspoon ground ginger
- Pinch ground cloves
- 1 tablespoon unsalted butter, divided
- 8 slices white bread

DIRECTIONS
1. In a large bowl, whisk together the eggs, rice milk, orange juice, cinnamon, ginger, and cloves until well blended.

2. In a large skillet over medium-high heat, melt half the butter.

3. Dredge four of the bread slices in the egg mixture until well soaked, and place them in the skillet.

4. Cook until golden brown on both sides, turning once, about 6 minutes total.

5. Repeat with the remaining butter and bread.

6. Serve 2 pieces of hot French toast to each person.

NUTRITION PER SERVING: Calories: 237; Total fat: 10g; Saturated fat: 4g; Cholesterol: 220mg; Sodium: 84mg; Carbohydrates: 27g; Fiber: 1g; Phosphorus: 119mg; Potassium: 158mg; Protein: 11g

7. Breakfast Tacos

Preparation Time: 10 minutes
Cooking Time: 10 minutes
Servings: 4
Difficulty: Easy
INGREDIENTS
- 1 teaspoon olive oil
- ½ sweet onion, chopped
- ½ red bell pepper, chopped
- ½ teaspoon minced garlic
- 4 eggs, beaten
- ½ teaspoon ground cumin
- Pinch red pepper flakes
- 4 tortillas
- ¼ cup tomato salsa

DIRECTIONS

1. In a large skillet over medium-high heat, heat the olive oil.
2. Add the onion, bell pepper, and garlic, and sauté until softened, about 5 minutes.
3. Add the eggs, cumin, and red pepper flakes, and scramble the eggs with the vegetables until cooked through and fluffy.
4. Spoon one-fourth of the egg mixture into the center of each tortilla, and top each with 1 tablespoon of salsa.
5. Serve immediately.

NUTRITION PER SERVING: Calories: 210; Total fat: 6g; Saturated fat: 2g; Cholesterol: 211mg; Sodium: 346mg; Carbohydrates: 17g; Fiber: 1g; Phosphorus: 120mg; Potassium: 141mg; Protein: 9g

8. Baked Egg Casserole

Preparation Time: 15 minutes
Cooking Time: 30 minutes
Servings: 4
Difficulty: Easy
INGREDIENTS
- 1 teaspoon olive oil, plus more for the baking dish
- ½ sweet onion, chopped
- ½ red bell pepper, chopped
- ½ teaspoon minced jalapeño pepper
- ½ teaspoon minced garlic
- 1 cup chopped fresh spinach
- Freshly ground black pepper
- 8 eggs, beaten
- 1 tablespoon chopped fresh parsley
DIRECTIONS

1. Preheat the oven to 375°F.
2. Lightly coat an 8-by-8-inch baking dish with olive oil.
3. In a large skillet over medium-high heat, heat 1 teaspoon of olive oil.
4. Sauté the onion, bell pepper, jalapeño pepper, and garlic until softened, about 5 minutes.
5. Add the spinach, and sauté until wilted, about 3 minutes.
6. Season the vegetables with black pepper. Transfer to the prepared baking dish.
7. Pour the eggs over the vegetables, and sprinkle with the parsley.
8. Bake until the eggs are firm, about 20 minutes.

Cut into 4 servings and serve.

NUTRITION PER SERVING: Calories: 128; Total fat: 7g; Saturated fat: 2g; Cholesterol: 282mg; Sodium: 62mg; Carbohydrates: 2g; Fiber: 0g; Phosphorus: 120mg; Potassium: 140mg; Protein: 9g

9. Bell Pepper and Feta Crustless Quiche

Preparation Time: 15 minutes
Cooking Time: 25 minutes
Servings: 5
Difficulty: Easy
INGREDIENTS
- 1 teaspoon olive oil, plus more for the pie dish
- 1 small sweet onion, chopped
- 1 teaspoon minced garlic
- 1 red bell pepper, chopped

- 1 cup Homemade Rice Milk (here; or use unsweetened store-bought)
- 4 eggs
- ¼ cup all-purpose flour
- ¼ cup low-sodium feta cheese
- 2 tablespoons chopped fresh basil leaves
- Freshly ground black pepper

DIRECTIONS

1. Preheat the oven to 400°F.
2. Lightly coat a 9-inch pie plate with olive oil.
3. In a medium skillet over medium-high heat, heat 1 teaspoon of olive oil.
4. Add the onion and garlic, and sauté until softened, about 3 minutes.
5. Stir in the bell pepper, and sauté about 3 minutes.
6. Transfer the vegetables to the prepared pie plate.
7. In a medium bowl, whisk together the rice milk, eggs, and flour until blended.
8. Stir in the feta cheese and basil, and season with black pepper.
9. Pour the egg mixture over the vegetables in the pie plate. Bake until the center is set and the edge is golden brown, about 20 minutes.
10. Serve hot, warm, or cold.

NUTRITION PER SERVING: Calories: 172; Total fat: 5g; Saturated fat: 3g; Cholesterol: 179mg; Sodium: 154mg; Carbohydrates: 20g; Fiber: 1g; Phosphorus: 120mg; Potassium: 122mg; Protein: 8g

10. Egg White and Broccoli Omelet

Preparation Time: 5 minutes
Cooking Time: 4 minutes
Servings: 2
Difficulty: Easy
INGREDIENTS

- 4 egg whites
- 1/3 cup of boiled broccoli
- ½ teaspoon of Dill
- 1 tablespoon of parmesan cheese, grated
- Salt/Pepper

DIRECTIONS

1. In a small bowl, beat together the egg whites until stiff and white.
2. Add the dill, the broccoli, and the parmesan cheese and incorporate everything with a spatula (do not over whisk).
3. Spray the pan with a bit of cooking spray and pour the egg and broccoli mixture. Cook around 1-2 minutes on each side.
4. Turn the omelet in half and optionally garnish with just a little bit of cheese on top.

NUTRITION: Calories: 56.82 kcal Carbohydrate: 2.7 g Protein: 10.57 g Sodium: 271.9 mg Potassium: 168.74 mg Phosphorus: 50.8 mg Dietary Fiber: 0.79 g Fat: 1.65 g

11. Yogurt Parfait with Strawberries

Preparation Time: 5 minutes
Cooking Time: 1 minute
Servings: 2
Difficulty: Easy
INGREDIENTS

- ½ cup of soy yogurt (plain)
- 1 scoop of vanilla flavored protein
- 5 fresh strawberries, sliced
- 1 tablespoon of agave syrup

DIRECTIONS

1. In a bowl, slowly whisk the protein powder with the yogurt.
2. Add the strawberry slices and the agave syrup on top.
3. Serve.

NUTRITION: Calories: 153.25 kcal Carbohydrate: 23.5 g Protein: 12.67 g Sodium: 93.32 mg Potassium: 85.9 mg Phosphorus: 62.75 mg Dietary Fiber: 1.43 g Fat: 1.17 g

12. Mexican Scrambled Eggs in Tortilla

Preparation Time: 5 minutes
Cooking Time: 2 minutes
Servings: 2
Difficulty: Easy
INGREDIENTS

- 2 medium corn tortillas
- 4 egg whites
- 1 teaspoon of cumin
- 3 teaspoons of green chilies, diced
- ½ teaspoon of hot pepper sauce
- 2 tablespoons of salsa
- ½ teaspoon salt

DIRECTIONS

1. Spray some cooking spray on a medium skillet and heat for a few seconds.
2. Whisk the eggs with the green chilies, hot sauce, and comminute
3. Add the eggs into the pan, and whisk with a spatula to scramble. Add the salt.
4. Cook until fluffy and done (1-2 minutes) over low heat.
5. Open the tortillas and spread 1 tablespoon of salsa on each.
6. Distribute the egg mixture onto the tortillas and wrap gently to make a burrito.
7. Serve warm.

NUTRITION: Calories: 44.1 kcal Carbohydrate: 2.23 g Protein: 7.69 g Sodium: 854 mg Potassium: 189 mg Phosphorus: 22 mg Dietary Fiber: 0.5 g Fat: 0.39 g

13. American Blueberry Pancakes

Preparation Time: 5 minutes
Cooking Time: 10 minutes
Servings: 6
Difficulty: medium
INGREDIENTS

- 1 ½ cups of all-purpose flour, sifted
- 1 cup of buttermilk
- 3 tablespoons of sugar

- 2 tablespoons of unsalted butter, melted
- 2 teaspoon of baking powder
- 2 eggs, beaten
- 1 cup of canned blueberries, rinsed

DIRECTIONS

1. Combine the flour, baking powder and sugar in a bowl.
2. Make a hole in the center and slowly add the rest of the ingredients.
3. Begin to stir gently from the sides to the center with a spatula, until you get a smooth and creamy batter.
4. Spray a small pan with cooking spray and place over medium heat.
5. Take one measuring cup and fill 1/3rd of its capacity with the batter to make each pancake.
6. Use a spoon to pour the pancake batter and let cook until golden brown. Flip once to cook the other side.
7. Serve warm with optional agave syrup.

NUTRITION: Calories: 251.69 kcal Carbohydrate: 41.68 g Protein: 7.2 g Sodium: 186.68 mg Potassium: 142.87 mg Phosphorus: 255.39 mg Dietary Fiber: 1.9 g Fat: 6.47 g

14. Raspberry Peach Breakfast Smoothie

Preparation Time: 5 minutes
Cooking Time: 1 minute
Difficulty: medium
Servings: 2

INGREDIENTS

- 1/3 cup of raspberries, (it can be frozen)
- 1/2 peach, skin and pit removed
- 1 tablespoon of honey
- 1 cup of coconut water

DIRECTIONS

1. Combine all the ingredients together in a blender until smooth.
2. Pour and serve chilled in a tall glass or mason jar.

NUTRITION: Calories: 86.3 kcal Carbohydrate: 20.6 g Protein: 1.4 g Sodium: 3 mg Potassium: 109 mg Phosphorus: 36.08 mg Dietary Fiber: 2.6 g Fat: 0.31 g

15. Fast Microwave Egg Scramble

Preparation Time: 5 minutes
Cooking Time: 1-2 minutes
Servings: 1
Difficulty: medium
INGREDIENTS

- 1 large egg
- 2 large egg whites
- 2 tablespoons of milk
- Kosher pepper, ground

DIRECTIONS

1. Spray a coffee cup with a bit of cooking spray.
2. Whisk all the ingredients together and place into the coffee cup.
3. Place the cup with the eggs into the microwave and set to cook for approx. 45 seconds. Take out and stir.

4. Return to the microwave and cook for another 30 seconds.
5. Serve.

NUTRITION: Calories: 128.6 kcal Carbohydrate: 2.47 g Protein: 12.96 g Sodium: 286.36 mg Potassium: 185.28 mg Phosphorus: 122.22 mg Dietary Fiber: 0 g Fat: 5.96 g

16. Mango Lassi Smoothie

Preparation Time: 5 minutes
Cooking Time: 0 minute
Servings: 2
Difficulty: medium
INGREDIENTS

- ½ cup of plain yogurt
- ½ cup of plain water
- ½ cup of sliced mango
- 1 tablespoon of sugar
- ¼ teaspoon of cardamom
- ¼ teaspoon cinnamon
- ¼ cup lime juice

DIRECTIONS

1. Pulse all the above **ingredients** in a blender until smooth (around 1 minute).
2. Pour into tall glasses or mason jars and serve chilled immediately.

NUTRITION: Calories: 89.02 kcal Carbohydrate: 14.31 g Protein: 2.54 g Sodium: 30 mg Potassium: 185.67 mg Phosphorus: 67.88 mg Dietary Fiber: 0.77 g Fat: 2.05 g

17. Breakfast Maple Sausage

Preparation Time: 15 minutes
Cooking Time: 8 minutes
Servings: 12
Difficulty: medium
INGREDIENTS

- 1 pound of pork, minced
- ½ pound lean turkey meat, ground
- ¼ teaspoon of nutmeg
- ½ teaspoon black pepper
- ¼ all spice
- 2 tablespoon of maple syrup
- 1 tablespoon of water

DIRECTIONS

1. Combine all the ingredients in a bowl.
2. Cover and place in the fridge for 3-4 hours.
3. Take the mixture and form into small flat patties with your hand (around 10-12 patties).
4. Lightly grease a medium skillet with oil and shallow fry the patties over medium to high heat, until brown (around 4-5 minutes on each side).
5. Serve hot.

NUTRITION: Calories: 53.85 kcal Carbohydrate: 2.42 g Protein: 8.5 g Sodium: 30.96 mg Potassium: 84.68 mg Phosphorus: 83.49 mg Dietary Fiber: 0.03 g Fat: 0.9 g

18. Summer Veggie Omelet

Preparation Time: 5 minutes
Cooking Time: 5 minutes

Servings: 2
Difficulty: medium
INGREDIENTS

- 4 large egg whites
- ¼ cup of sweet corn, frozen
- ⅓ cup of zucchini, grated
- 2 green onions, sliced
- 1 tablespoon of cream cheese
- Kosher pepper

DIRECTIONS

1. Grease a medium pan with some cooking spray and add the onions, corn and grated zucchini.
2. Sauté for a couple of minutes until softened.
3. Beat the eggs together with the water, cream cheese, and pepper in a bowl.
4. Add the eggs into the veggie mixture in the pan, and let cook while moving the edges from inside to outside with a spatula, to allow raw egg to cook through the edges.
5. Flip the omelet with the help of a dish (placed over the pan and flipped upside down and then back to the pan).
6. Let sit for another 1-2 minutes.
7. Fold in half and serve.

NUTRITION: Calories: 90 kcal Carbohydrate: 15.97 g Protein: 8.07 g Sodium: 227 mg Potassium: 244.24 mg Phosphorus: 45.32 mg Dietary Fiber: 0.88 g Fat: 2.44 g

19. Raspberry Overnight Porridge

Preparation Time: Overnight
Cooking Time: 0 minute
Servings: 12
Difficulty: medium
INGREDIENTS

- ⅓ cup of rolled oats
- ½ cup almond milk
- 1 tablespoon of honey
- 5-6 raspberries, fresh or canned and unsweetened
- ⅓ cup of rolled oats
- ½ cup almond milk
- 1 tablespoon of honey
- 5-6 raspberries, fresh or canned and unsweetened

DIRECTIONS

1. Combine the oats, almond milk, and honey in a mason jar and place into the fridge for overnight.
2. Serve the next morning with the raspberries on top.

NUTRITION: Calories: 143.6 kcal Carbohydrate: 34.62 g Protein: 3.44 g Sodium: 77.88 mg Potassium: 153.25 mg Phosphorus: 99.3 mg Dietary Fiber: 7.56 g Fat: 3.91 g

20. Cheesy Scrambled Eggs with Fresh Herbs

Preparation Time: 15 minutes
Cooking Time: 10 minutes
Servings: 4
Difficulty: medium

INGREDIENTS

- Eggs – 3
- Egg whites – 2
- Cream cheese – ½ cup
- Unsweetened rice milk – ¼ cup
- Chopped scallion – 1 Tablespoon green part only
- Chopped fresh tarragon – 1 Tablespoon
- Unsalted butter – 2 Tablespoons.
- Ground black pepper to taste

DIRECTIONS

1. In a bowl, whisk the eggs, egg whites, cream cheese, rice milk, scallions, and tarragon until mixed and smooth.
2. Melt the butter in a skillet.
3. Pour in the egg mixture and cook, stirring, for 5 minutes or until the eggs are thick and curds creamy.
4. Season with pepper and serve.

NUTRITION: Calories: 221 Fat: 19g Carb: 3g Phosphorus: 119mg Potassium: 140mg Sodium: 193mg Protein: 8g

21. Turkey and Spinach Scramble on Melba Toast

Preparation Time: 2 minutes
Cooking Time: 15 minutes
Servings: 2
Difficulty: medium
INGREDIENTS

- Extra virgin olive oil – 1 teaspoon
- Raw spinach – 1 cup
- Garlic – ½ clove, minced
- Nutmeg – 1 teaspoon grated
- Cooked and diced turkey breast – 1 cup
- Melba toast – 4 slices
- Balsamic vinegar – 1 teaspoon

DIRECTIONS

1. Heat a skillet over medium heat and add oil.
2. Add turkey and heat through for 6 to 8 minutes.
3. Add spinach, garlic, and nutmeg and stir-fry for 6 minutes more.
4. Plate up the Melba toast and top with spinach and turkey scramble.
5. Drizzle with balsamic vinegar and serve.

NUTRITION: Calories: 301 Fat: 19g Carb: 12g Phosphorus: 215mg Potassium: 269mg Sodium: 360mg Protein: 19g

22. Vegetable Omelet

Preparation Time: 15 minutes
Cooking Time: 10 minutes
Servings: 3
Difficulty: medium
INGREDIENTS

- Egg whites – 4
- Egg – 1
- Chopped fresh parsley – 2 Tablespoons.
- Water – 2 Tablespoons.
- Olive oil spray
- Chopped and boiled red bell pepper – ½ cup
- Chopped scallion – ¼ cup, both green and white parts
- Ground black pepper

DIRECTIONS

1. Whisk together the egg, egg whites, parsley, and water until well blended. Set aside.
2. Spray a skillet with olive oil spray and place over medium heat.
3. Sauté the peppers and scallion for 3 minutes or until softened.
4. Pour the egg mixture into the skillet over vegetables and cook, swirling the skillet, for 2 minutes or until the edges start to set. Cook until set.
5. Season with black pepper and serve.

NUTRITION: Calories: 77 Fat: 3g Carb: 2g Phosphorus: 67mg Potassium: 194mg Sodium: 229mg Protein: 12g

23. Breakfast Salad from Grains and Fruits

Preparation Time: 5 minutes
Cooking Time: 15 minutes
Servings: 6
Difficulty: hard
Ingredients:

- 1 8-oz low-fat vanilla yogurt
- 1 cup raisins
- 1 orange
- 1 delicious red apple
- 1 Granny Smith apple
- ¾ cup bulgur
- ¾ cup quick-cooking brown rice
- ¼ teaspoons salt
- 3 cups water

Direction:

1. On high fire, place a large pot and bring water to a boil.
2. Add bulgur and rice. Lower fire to a simmer and cooks for ten minutes while covered.
3. Turn off fire, set aside for 2 minutes while covered.
4. On a baking sheet, transfer and evenly spread grains to cool.
5. Meanwhile, peel oranges and cut them into sections. Chop and core apples.
6. Once grains are cool, transfer to a large serving bowl along with fruits.
7. Add yogurt and mix well to coat.
8. Serve and enjoy.

Nutrition: Calories: 187 Carbs: 4g Protein: 8g Fats: 3g Phosphorus: 45mg Potassium: 36mg Sodium: 117mg

24. French Toast with Applesauce

Preparation Time: 5 minutes
Cooking Time: 15 minutes
Servings: 6
Difficulty: medium
Ingredients:

- ¼ cup unsweetened applesauce
- ½ cup milk
- 1 teaspoons ground cinnamon
- 2 eggs
- 2 tablespoons white sugar
- 6 slices whole wheat bread

Directions:

1. Mix well applesauce, sugar, cinnamon, milk, and eggs in a mixing bowl.
2. Dip the bread into applesauce mixture until wet; take note that you should do this one slice at a time.

3.   On medium fire, heat a nonstick skillet greased with cooking spray.

4.   Add soaked bread one at a time and cook for 2-3 minutes per side or until lightly browned.

5.   Serve and enjoy.

Nutrition: Calories: 57 Carbs: 6g Protein: 4g Fats: 4g Phosphorus: 69mg Potassium: 88mg Sodium: 43mg

LUNCH

25. Bagels Made Healthy

Preparation Time: 5 minutes
Cooking Time: 25 minutes
Servings: 8
Difficulty: medium
Ingredients:

- 2 teaspoons yeast
- 1 ½ tablespoon olive oil
- 1 ¼ cups bread flour
- 2 cups whole wheat flour
- 1 tablespoon vinegar
- 2 tablespoons honey
- 1 ½ cups warm water

Directions:

1. In a bread machine, mix all the ingredients, and then process on dough cycle.
2. Once done or end of the cycle, create 8 pieces shaped like a flattened ball.
3. Using your thumb, you must create a hole at the center of each, and then create a donut shape.
4. Place the donut-shaped dough on a greased baking sheet, then covers and let it rise about ½ hour.
5. Prepare about 2 inches of water to boil in a large pan.
6. In boiling water, drop one at a time the bagels and boil for 1 minute, then turn them once.
7. Remove them and return them to a baking sheet and bake at 350oF (175oC) for about 20 to 25 minutes until golden brown.
Nutrition: Calories: 221 Carbs: 42g Protein: 7g Fats: 3g Phosphorus: 130mg Potassium: 166mg Sodium: 47mg

26. Cornbread with Southern Twist

Preparation Time: 15 minutes
Cooking Time: 60 minutes
Servings: 8
Difficulty: Easy
Ingredients:

- 2 tablespoons shortening
- 1 ¼ cups skim milk
- ¼ cup egg substitute
- 4 tablespoons sodium-free baking powder
- ½ cup flour
- 1 ½ cups cornmeal

Directions:

1. Prepare an 8x8-inch baking dish or a black iron skillet, and then add shortening.
2. Put the baking dish or skillet inside the oven at 425 ºF; once the shortening has melted, that means the pan is hot already.
3. In a bowl, add milk and egg, and then mix well.
4. Take out the skillet, and add the melted shortening into the batter and stir well.

5. Pour mixture into skillet after mixing all the ingredients.

6. Cook the cornbread for 15-20 minutes until it is golden brown.

Nutrition: Calories: 166 Carbs: 35g Protein: 5g Fats: 1g Phosphorus: 79mg Potassium: 122mg Sodium: 34mg

27. Grandma's Pancake Special

Preparation Time: 5 minutes
Cooking Time: 15 minutes
Servings: 3
Difficulty: Easy
Ingredients:

- 1 tablespoon oil
- 1 cup milk
- 1 egg
- 2 teaspoons sodium-free baking powder
- 2 tablespoons sugar
- 1 ¼ cups flour

Directions:

1. Mix together all the dry **ingredients**, such as the flour, sugar, and baking powder.

2. Combine oil, milk, and egg in another bowl. Once done, add them all to the flour mixture.

3. Make sure that as you stir the mixture; blend them together until slightly lumpy.

4. In a hot, greased griddle, pour-in at least ¼ cup of the batter to make each pancake.

5. To cook, ensure that the bottom is a bit brown, then turn and cook the other side as well.

Nutrition: Calories: 167 Carbs: 50g Protein: 11g Fats: 11g Phosphorus: 176mg Potassium: 215mg Sodium: 70mg

28. Pasta with Indian Lentils

Preparation Time: 5 minutes
Cooking Time: 0 minutes
Servings: 6
Difficulty: Easy
Ingredients:

- ¼-½ cup fresh cilantro (chopped)
- 3 cups water
- 2 small dry red peppers (whole)
- 1 teaspoons turmeric
- 1 teaspoons ground cumin
- 2-3 cloves garlic (minced)
- 1 can diced tomatoes (w/juice)
- 1 large onion (chopped)
- ½ cup dry lentils (rinsed)
- ½ cup orzo or tiny pasta

Directions:

1. Combine all the ingredients in the skillet except for the cilantro, and then boil on medium-high heat.

2. Ensure to cover and slightly reduce heat to medium-low and simmer until pasta is tender for about 35 minutes.

3. Afterwards, take out the chili peppers, then add cilantro and top it with low-fat sour cream.

Nutrition: Calories: 175 Carbs: 40g Protein: 3g Fats: 2g Phosphorus: 139mg Potassium: 513mg Sodium: 61mg

29.   Mexican Style Burritos

Preparation Time: 5 minutes
Cooking Time: 15 minutes
Servings: 2
Difficulty: Easy
Ingredients:
- Olive oil – 1 tablespoon
- Corn tortillas – 2
- Red onion – ¼ cup, chopped
- Red bell peppers – ¼ cup, chopped
- Red chili – ½, deseeded and chopped
- Eggs – 2
- Juice of 1 lime
- Cilantro – 1 tablespoon chopped

Directions:
1.   Turn the broiler to medium heat and place the tortillas underneath for 1 to 2 minutes on each side or until lightly toasted.
2.   Remove and keep the broiler on.
3.   Sauté onion, chili and bell peppers for 5 to 6 minutes or until soft.
4.   Place the eggs on top of the onions and peppers and place skillet under the broiler for 5-6 minutes or until the eggs are cooked.
5.   Serve half the eggs and vegetables on top of each tortilla and sprinkle with cilantro and lime juice to serve.

Nutrition: Calories: 202 Fat: 13g Carb: 19g Phosphorus: 184mg Potassium: 233mg Sodium: 77mg Protein: 9g

30.   Sweet Pancakes

Preparation Time: 10 minutes
Cooking Time: 5 minutes
Servings: 5
Difficulty: Easy
Ingredients:
- All-purpose flour – 1 cup
- Granulated sugar – 1 tablespoon
- Baking powder – 2 teaspoons.
- Egg whites – 2
- Almond milk - 1 cup
- Olive oil - 2 tablespoons.
- Maple extract – 1 tablespoon

Directions:
1.   Combine the flour, sugar and baking powder in a bowl.
2.   Make a well in the center and place to one side.
3.   Mix the egg whites, milk, oil, and maple extract, do this in another bowl.
4.   Add the egg mixture to the well and gently mix until a batter is formed.
5.   Heat skillet over medium heat.
6.   Cook 2 minutes on each side or until the pancake is golden only add 1/5 of the batter to the pan.
7.   Repeat with the remaining batter and serve.

Nutrition: Calories: 178 Potassium: 126mg Sodium: 297mg Protein: 6g

31.   Buckwheat and Grapefruit Porridge

Preparation Time: 5 minutes
Cooking Time: 20 minutes

Servings: 2
Difficulty: Easy
Ingredients:
- Buckwheat – ½ cup
- Grapefruit – ¼, chopped
- Honey – 1 tablespoon
- Almond milk – 1 ½ cups
- Water – 2 cups

Directions:
1. Boil water on the stove. Add the buckwheat and place the lid on the pan.
2. Simmer for 7 to 10 minutes, in a low heat. Check to ensure water does not dry out.
3. Remove and set aside for 5 minutes, do this when most of the water is absorbed.
4. Drain excess water from the pan and stir in almond milk, heating through for 5 minutes.
5. Add the honey and grapefruit.
6. Serve.

Nutrition: Calories: 231 Fat: 4g Carb: 43g Phosphorus: 165mg Potassium: 370mg Sodium: 135mg

32. Egg and Veggie Muffins

Preparation Time: 15 minutes
Cooking Time: 20 minutes
Servings: 4
Difficulty: Easy
Ingredients:
- Cooking spray
- Eggs – 4
- Unsweetened rice milk – 2 tablespoons
- Sweet onion – ½, chopped
- Red bell pepper – ½, chopped
- Pinch red pepper flakes
- Pinch ground black pepper

Directions:
1. Preheat the oven to 350f.
2. Spray 4 muffin pans with cooking spray. Set aside.
3. Whisk together the milk, eggs, onion, red pepper, parsley, red pepper flakes, and black pepper until mixed.
4. Pour the egg mixture into prepared muffin pans.
5. Bake until the muffins are puffed and golden, about 18 to 20 minutes.
6. Serve

Nutrition: Calories: 84 Fat: 5g Carb: 3g Phosphorus: 110mg Potassium: 117mg Sodium: 75mg Protein: 7g

33. Cherry Berry Bulgur Bowl

Preparation Time: 15 minutes
Cooking Time: 15 minutes
Servings: 4
Difficulty: Easy
Ingredients:
- 1 cup medium-grind bulgur
- 2 cups water
- Pinch salt
- 1 cup halved and pitted cherries or 1 cup canned cherries, drained
- ½ cup raspberries
- ½ cup blackberries
- 1 tablespoon cherry jam
- 2 cups plain whole-milk yogurt

Directions:

1. Mix the bulgur, water, and salt in a medium saucepan. Do this in a medium heat. Bring to a boil.

2. Reduce the heat to low and simmer, partially covered, for 12 to 15 minutes or until the bulgur is almost tender. Cover, and let stand for 5 minutes to finish cooking do this after removing the pan from the heat.

3. While the bulgur is cooking, combine the raspberries and blackberries in a medium bowl. Stir the cherry jam into the fruit.

4. When the bulgur is tender, divide among four bowls. Top each bowl with ½ cup of yogurt and an equal amount of the berry mixture and serve.

Nutrition: Calories: 242 Total Fat: 6g Saturated Fat: 3g Sodium: 85mg Phosphorus: 237mg Potassium: 438mg Carbohydrates: 44g Fiber: 7g Protein: 9g Sugar: 13g

34. Sausage Breakfast Casserole

Preparation Time: 10 minutes
Cooking Time: 50 minutes
Servings: 8
Difficulty: Easy
Ingredients:
- 12 eggs
- 1 lb. ground Italian sausage
- 2 ½ tomatoes, sliced
- 3 tbsp. coconut flour
- ¼ cup coconut milk
- 2 small zucchinis, shredded
- Pepper to taste
- Salt to taste

Directions:
1. Preheat the oven to 350ºF.
2. Spray casserole dish with cooking spray and set aside.
3. Cook sausage in a pan until brown.
4. Transfer sausage to a mixing bowl.
5. Add coconut flour, milk, eggs, zucchini, pepper, and salt. Stir well.
6. Add eggs and whisk to combine.
7. Transfer bowl mixture into the casserole dish and top with tomato slices.
8. Bake for 50 minutes.
9. Serve and enjoy.

Nutrition: Calories 305 Fat 21.8g Carbohydrates 6.3g Sugar 3.3g Protein 19.6g Cholesterol 286mg

35. Chicken Wild Rice Soup

Preparation time: 10 minutes
Cooking time: 15 minutes
Servings: 6
Difficulty: Easy
INGREDIENTS
- 2/3 cup wild rice, uncooked
- 1 tablespoon onion, chopped finely
- 1 tablespoon fresh parsley, chopped
- 1 cup carrots, chopped
- 8-ounce chicken breast, cooked
- 2 tablespoon butter

- 1/4 cup all-purpose white flour
- 5 cups low-sodium chicken broth
- 1 tablespoon slivered almonds

DIRECTIONS

1. Start by adding rice and 2 cups broth along with ½ cup water to a cooking pot.
2. Cook until the rice is al dente and set it aside.
3. Add butter to a saucepan and melt it.
4. Stir in onion and sauté until soft then add the flour and the remaining broth.
5. Stir and cook for 1 minute then add the chicken, cooked rice, and carrots.
6. Cook for 5 minutes on simmer.
7. Garnish with almonds.
8. Serve fresh.

NUTRITION: Calories 287. Protein 21 g. Carbohydrates 35 g. Fat 7 g. Cholesterol 42 mg. Sodium 182 mg. Potassium 384 mg. Phosphorus 217 mg. Calcium 45 mg. Fiber 1.6 g.

36. Chicken Noodle Soup

Preparation time: 10 minutes
Cooking time: 25 minutes
Servings: 2
Difficulty: Easy
INGREDIENTS

- 1 1/2 cups low-sodium vegetable broth
- 1 cup of water
- 1/4 teaspoon poultry seasoning
- 1/4 teaspoon black pepper
- 1 cup chicken strips
- 1/4 cup carrot
- 2-ounce egg noodles, uncooked

DIRECTIONS

1. Toss all the ingredients into a slow cooker
2. Cook soup on high heat for 25 minutes.
3. Serve warm.

NUTRITION: Calories 103. Protein 8 g. Carbohydrates 11 g. Fat 3 g. Cholesterol 4 mg. Sodium 355 mg. Potassium 264 mg. Phosphorus 128 mg. Calcium 46 mg. Fiber 4.0 g.

37. Cucumber Soup

Preparation time: 10 minutes
Cooking time: 0 minutes
Servings: 4
Difficulty: Easy
INGREDIENTS

- 2 medium cucumbers, peeled and diced
- 1/3 cup sweet white onion, diced

- 1 green onion, diced
- 1/4 cup fresh mint
- 2 tablespoon fresh dill
- 2 tablespoon lemon juice
- 2/3 cup water
- 1/2 cup half and half cream
- 1/3 cup sour cream
- 1/2 teaspoon pepper
- Fresh dill sprigs for garnish

DIRECTIONS

1. Toss all the ingredients into a food processor.
2. Puree the mixture and refrigerate for 2 hours.
3. Garnish with dill sprigs.
4. Enjoy fresh.

NUTRITION: Calories 77. Protein 2 g. Carbohydrates 6 g. Fat 5 g. Cholesterol 12 mg. Sodium 128 mg. Potassium 258 mg. Phosphorus 64 mg. Calcium 60 mg. Fiber 1.0 g.

38. Squash and Turmeric Soup

Preparation time: 10 minutes
Cooking time: 30 minutes
Servings: 4
Difficulty: Easy
INGREDIENTS

- 4 cups low-sodium vegetable broth
- 2 medium zucchini squash, peeled and diced
- 2 medium yellow crookneck squash, peeled and diced
- 1 small onion, diced
- 1/2 cup frozen green peas
- 2 tablespoon olive oil
- 1/2 cup plain nonfat Greek yogurt
- 2 teaspoon turmeric

DIRECTIONS

1. Warm the broth in a saucepan on medium heat.
2. Toss in onion, squash, and zucchini.
3. Let it simmer for approximately 25 minutes then add oil and green peas.
4. Cook for another 5 minutes then allow it to cool.
5. Puree the soup using a handheld blender then add Greek yogurt and turmeric.
6. Refrigerate it overnight and serve fresh.

NUTRITION: Calories 100. Protein 4 g. Carbohydrates 10 g. Fat 5 g. Cholesterol 1 mg. Sodium 279 mg. Potassium 504 mg. Phosphorus 138 mg. Calcium 60 mg. Fiber 2.8 g.

39. Leek, Potato and Carrot Soup

Preparation time: 15min
Cooking time: 25min
Servings: 4
Difficulty: Easy
INGREDIENTS

- 1 - leek
- ¾ - cup diced and boiled potatoes
- ¾ - cup diced and boiled carrots
- 1 - garlic clove
- 1 - tablespoon oil
- crushed pepper to taste

- 3 - cups low sodium chicken stock
- chopped parsley for garnish
- 1 - bay leaf
- ¼ - teaspoon ground cumin

DIRECTIONS

1. Trim off and take away a portion of the coarse inexperienced portions of the leek, at that factor reduce daintily and flush altogether in virus water.
2. Channel properly. Warmth the oil in an extensively based pot.
3. Include the leek and garlic, and sear over low warmth for two-3 minutes, till sensitive.
4. Include the inventory, inlet leaf, cumin, and pepper. Heat the mixture to the point of boiling, mixing constantly.
5. Include the bubbled potatoes and carrots and stew for 10-15minutes
6. Modify the flavoring, eliminate the inlet leaf and serve sprinkled generously with slashed parsley.
7. To make a pureed soup, manner the soup in a blender or nourishment processor till smooth
8. Come again to the pan. Include ½ field milk.
9. Bring to bubble and stew for 2-3minutes

NUTRITION: Calories 315g, Fat 8g, Carbs 15g, Sugars 1.2g, Protein 26g

40. Roasted Red Pepper Soup

Preparation time: 30min

Cooking time: 35min
Servings: 4
Difficulty: Easy
INGREDIENTS

- 4 - cups low-sodium chicken broth
- 3 - red peppers
- 2 - medium onions
- 3 - tablespoon lemon juice
- 1 - tablespoon finely minced lemon zest
- A pinch cayenne peppers
- ¼ - teaspoon cinnamon
- ½ - cup finely minced fresh cilantro

DIRECTIONS

1. In a medium stockpot, consolidate each one of the fixings except for the cilantro and warmth to the point of boiling over excessive warm temperature.
2. Diminish the warmth and stew, ordinarily secured, for around 30 minutes, till thickened.
3. Cool marginally. Utilizing a hand blender or nourishment processor, puree the soup.
4. Include the cilantro and tenderly heat.

NUTRITION: Calories 265g, Fat 8g, Carbs 5g, Sugars 0.1g, Protein 29g

41. Yucatan Soup

Preparation time: 10 minutes
Cooking time: 20 minutes
Servings: 4
Difficulty: Easy
INGREDIENTS

- ½ cup onion, chopped
- 8 cloves garlic, chopped
- 2 Serrano chili peppers, chopped
- 1 medium tomato, chopped
- 1 ½ cups chicken breast, cooked, shredded
- 2 six-inch corn tortillas, sliced
- Nonstick cooking spray
- 1 tablespoon olive oil
- 4 cups chicken broth
- 1 bay leaf
- ¼ cup lime juice
- ¼ cup cilantro, chopped
- 1 teaspoon black pepper

DIRECTIONS

1. Spread the corn tortillas in a baking sheet and bake them for 3 minutes at 400ºF.
2. Place a suitably-sized saucepan over medium heat and add oil to heat.
3. Toss in chili peppers, garlic, and onion, then sauté until soft.
4. Stir in broth, tomatoes, bay leaf, and chicken.
5. Let this chicken soup cook for 10 minutes on a simmer.
6. Stir in cilantro, lime juice, and black pepper.
7. Garnish with baked corn tortillas.
8. Serve.

NUTRITION: Calories: 214 Protein: 20 g Carbohydrates: 12 g Fat: 10 g Cholesterol: 32 mg Sodium: 246 mg Potassium: 355 mg Phosphorus: 176 mg Calcium: 47 mg Fiber: 1.6 g

42. Zesty Taco Soup

Preparation time: 10 minutes
Cooking time: 7 hours
Servings: 2
Difficulty: Easy
INGREDIENTS

- 1 ½ pounds boneless skinless chicken breast
- 15 ½ ounces canned dark red kidney beans
- 15 ½ ounces canned white corn
- 1 cup canned tomatoes, diced
- ½ cup onion
- 15 ½ ounces canned yellow hominy
- ½ cup green bell peppers
- 1 garlic clove
- 1 medium jalapeno
- 1 tablespoon package McCormick
- 2 cups chicken broth

DIRECTIONS

1. Add drained beans, hominy, corn, onion, garlic, jalapeno pepper, chicken, and green peppers to a Crockpot.
2. Cover the beans-corn mixture and cook for 1 hour on High temperature.
3. Reduce the heat to LOW and continue cooking for 6 hours.
4. Shred the slow-cooked chicken and return to the taco soup.
5. Serve warm.

NUTRITION: Calories: 190 Protein: 21 g Carbohydrates: 19 g Fat: 3 g Cholesterol: 42 mg Sodium: 421 mg Potassium: 444 mg

Phosphorus: 210 mg Calcium: 28 mg Fiber: 4.3 g

43. Southwestern Posole

Preparation time: 10 minutes
Cooking time: 53 minutes
Servings: 4
Difficulty: Easy
INGREDIENTS

- 1 tablespoon olive oil
- 1-pound pork loin, diced
- ½ cup onion, chopped
- 1 garlic clove, chopped
- 28 ounces canned white hominy
- 4 ounces canned diced green chilis
- 4 cups chicken broth
- ¼ teaspoon black pepper

DIRECTIONS

1. Place a suitably-sized cooking pot over medium heat and add oil to heat.
2. Toss in pork pieces and sauté for 4 minutes.
3. Stir in garlic and onion, then stir for 4 minutes, or until onion is soft.
4. Add the remaining **ingredients**, then cover the pork soup.
5. Cook for 45 minutes, or until the pork is tender.
6. Serve warm.

NUTRITION: Calories: 286 Protein: 26 g Carbohydrates: 15 g Fat: 13 g Cholesterol: 63 mg Sodium: 399 mg Potassium: 346 mg Phosphorus: 182 mg Calcium: 31 mg Fiber: 3.4 g

44. Wild Rice Asparagus Soup

Preparation Time: 10 minutes
Cooking Time: 30 minutes
Servings: 4
Difficulty: Easy
Ingredients:

- 3/4 cup wild rice
- 2 cups asparagus, chopped
- 1 cup carrots, diced
- 1/2 cup onion, diced
- 3 garlic cloves, minced
- 1/4 cup unsalted butter
- 1/2 tsp thyme
- 1/2 tsp fresh ground pepper
- 1/4 tsp nutmeg
- 1 bay leaf
- 1/2 cup all-purpose flour
- 4 cups low-sodium chicken broth
- 1/2 cup extra dry vermouth
- 2 cups cooked chicken
- 4 cups unsweetened almond milk, unenriched

Directions:

1. Cook the wild rice as per the cooking instructions on the box or bag and drain.
2. Melt the butter in a Dutch oven and sauté garlic and onion.
3. Once soft, add spices, herbs, and carrots.
4. Cook on medium heat right until veggies are tender then add flour and stir cook for 10 minutes on low heat.
5. Add 4 cups of broth and vermouth and blend using a handheld blender.

6.   Dice the chicken pieces and add asparagus and chicken to the soup.

7.   Stir in almond milk and cook for 20 minutes.

8.   Add the wild rice and serve warm.

Nutrition: Calories 295. Protein 21 g. Carbohydrates 28 g. Fat 11 g. Cholesterol 45 mg. Sodium 385 mg. Potassium 527 mg. Phosphorus 252 mg. Calcium 183 mg. Fiber 3.3

45.   Nutmeg Chicken Soup

Preparation Time: 10 minutes
Cooking Time: 20 minutes
Servings: 4
Difficulty: Easy
Ingredients:

- 1 lb. boneless, skinless chicken breasts, uncooked
- 1 1/2 cups onion, sliced
- 1 1/2 cups celery, chopped
- 1 tbsp. olive oil
- 1 cup fresh carrots, chopped
- 1 cup fresh green beans, chopped
- 3 tbsp. all-purpose white flour
- 1 tsp dried oregano
- 2 tsp dried basil
- 1/4 tsp nutmeg
- 1 tsp thyme
- 32 oz. reduced-sodium chicken broth
- 1/2 cup 1% low-fat milk
- 2 cups frozen green peas
- 1/4 tsp black pepper

Directions:

1.   Add chicken to a skillet and sauté for 6 minutes then remove it from the heat.

2.   Warm up olive oil in a pan and sauté onion for 5 minutes.

3.   Stir in green beans, carrots, chicken, basil, oregano, flour, thyme, and nutmeg.

4.   Sauté for 3 minutes then transfer the ingredients to a large pan.

5.   Add milk and broth and cook until it boils.

6.   Stir in green peas and cook for 5 minutes.

7.   Adjust seasoning with pepper and serve warm.

Nutrition: Calories 131. Protein 14 g. Carbohydrates 12 g. Fat 3 g. Cholesterol 32 mg. Sodium 343 mg. Potassium 467 mg. Phosphorus 171 mg. Calcium 67 mg. Fiber 2.8 g.

46.   Hungarian Cherry Soup

Preparation Time: 10 minutes
Cooking Time: 15 minutes
Servings: 4
Difficulty: Easy
Ingredients:

- 1 1/2 cup fresh cherries
- 3 cups water
- 1/3 cup sugar
- 1/16 tsp salt
- 1 tbsp. all-purpose white flour
- 1/2 cup reduced-fat sour cream

Directions:

1.   Warm the water in a saucepan and add cherries and sugar.

2.   Let it boil then simmer for 10 minutes.

3. Remove 2 tbsp. of the cooking liquid and keep it aside.

4. Separate ¼ cup of liquid in a bowl and allow it to cool.

5. Add flour and sour cream to this liquid.

6. Mix well then return the mixture to the saucepan.

7. Cook for 5 minutes on low heat.

8. Garnish the soup with the reserved 2 tbsp. of liquid.

9. Serve and enjoy.

Nutrition: Calories 144. Protein 2 g. Carbohydrates 25 g. Fat 4 g. Cholesterol 12 mg. Sodium 57 mg. Potassium 144 mg. Phosphorus 40 mg. Calcium 47 mg. Fiber 1.0 g.

47. Italian Wedding Soup

Preparation Time: 10 minutes
Cooking Time: 10 minutes
Servings: 4
Difficulty: Easy
Ingredients:
- 1 lb. lean ground beef
- 2 eggs
- 1/4 cup dried bread crumbs
- 2 tbsp. parmesan cheese, grated
- 1 tsp dried basil
- 3 tbsp. onion, chopped
- 2 1/2 quarts low-sodium chicken broth
- 1 cup fresh spinach leaves
- 1 cup acini de pepe pasta, uncooked
- 3/4 cup carrots, chopped

Directions:

1. Start by tossing the eggs, beef, cheese, crumbs, onion, and basil in a bowl.

2. Mix it well then, a make a half-inch thick log and slice it into 80 pieces.

3. Roll the meat slices into meatballs.

4. Warm the broth in a stockpot then add pasta, spinach, carrots, and meatballs.

5. Bring it to a boil then simmer for 10 minutes on low heat.

6. Once it's done, serve warm.

Nutrition: Calories 165. Protein 21 g. Carbohydrates 11 g. Fat 6 g. Cholesterol 73 mg. Sodium 276 mg. Potassium 360 mg. Phosphorus 176 mg. Calcium 42 mg. Fiber 1.0 g.

48. Old Fashioned Salmon Soup

Preparation Time: 10 minutes
Cooking Time: 20 minutes
Servings: 4
Difficulty: Easy
Ingredients:
- 2 tbsp. unsalted butter
- 1 medium carrot, diced
- 1/2 cup celery, chopped
- 1/2 cup onion, sliced
- 1 lb. sockeye salmon, cooked, diced
- 2 cups reduced-sodium chicken broth
- 2 cups 1% low-fat milk
- 1/8 tsp black pepper
- 1/4 cup cornstarch
- 1/4 cup water

Directions:

1. Melt butter in a saucepan and sauté all the vegetables in it until soft.
2. Stir in salmon chunks, milk, pepper, and broth.
3. Bring it to boil then simmer on low heat.
4. Mix cornstarch with water in a bowl and add this slurry to the soup.
5. Cook and stir continuously until it thickens.
6. Serve fresh and warm.

Nutrition: Calories 155. Protein 14 g. Carbohydrates 9 g. Fat 7 g. Cholesterol 37 mg. Sodium 113 mg. Potassium 369 mg. Phosphorus 218 mg. Calcium 92 mg. Fiber 0.5 g

1. Start by adding olive oil, flour, and the bouillon cubes to a saucepan.
2. Add water 3/4 of the way up the saucepan and let it boil.
3. Stir in peppers, vinegar, and oxtails.
4. Cover it and cook until the oxtails soften.
5. Add all vegetables including, celery, and onion to the soup.
6. Cook until the veggies soften.
7. Serve fresh and warm.

Nutrition: Calories 313. Protein 21 g. Carbohydrates 10 g. Fat 21 g. Cholesterol 66 mg. Sodium 325 mg. Potassium 596 mg. Phosphorus 257 mg. Calcium 61 mg. Fiber 2.2 g.

49. Oxtail Soup

Preparation Time: 10 minutes
Cooking Time: 20 minutes
Servings: 4
Difficulty: Easy
Ingredients:

- 1 medium bell pepper, diced
- 1 small jalapeno pepper, diced
- 1 large onion, sliced
- 3 celery stalks, chopped
- 1 tbsp. olive oil
- 1 tbsp. all-purpose white flour
- 2 bouillon cubes
- 2-lb package oxtail
- 1 tbsp. vinegar
- 1/4 tsp black pepper
- 1/2 tsp herb seasoning blend
- 12 oz. frozen gumbo vegetables

Directions:

50. Classic Chicken Soup

Preparation Time: 5-10 minutes
Cooking Time: 35 minutes
Serving: 1
Difficulty: Easy
Ingredients:

- 2 teaspoons minced garlic
- 2 celery stalks, chopped
- 1 tablespoon unsalted butter
- ½ sweet onion, diced
- 1 carrot, diced
- 4 cups water
- 1 teaspoon chopped fresh thyme
- 2 cups chopped cooked chicken breast
- 1 cup chicken stock
- Black pepper (ground), to taste
- 2 tablespoons chopped fresh parsley

Directions:

1. Take a medium-large cooking pot, heat oil over medium heat.

2. Add onion and stir-cook until it becomes translucent and softened.

3. Add garlic and stir-cook until it becomes fragrant.

4. Add celery, carrot, chicken, chicken stock, and water.

5. Boil the mixture.

6. Over low heat, simmer the mixture for about 25-30 minutes until veggies are tender.

7. Mix in thyme and cook for 2 minutes. Season to taste with black pepper.

8. Serve warm with parsley on top.

Nutrition: Calories: 135; Fat: 6g Phosphorus: 122mg Potassium: 208mg Sodium: 74mg Carbohydrates: 3g Protein: 15g.

51. Beef Okra Soup

Preparation Time: 10 minutes
Cooking Time: 45-55 minutes
Serving: 1
Difficulty: Easy
Ingredients:

- ½ cup okra
- ½ teaspoon basil
- ½ cup carrots, diced
- 3 ½ cups water
- 1-pound beef stew meat
- 1 cup raw sliced onions
- ½ cup green peas
- 1 teaspoon black pepper
- ½ teaspoon thyme
- ½ cup corn kernels

Directions:

1. Take a medium-large cooking pot, heat oil over medium heat.

2. Add water, beef stew meat, black pepper, onions, basil, thyme, and stir-cook for 40-45 minutes until meat is tender.

3. Add all veggies. Over low heat, simmer the mixture for about 20-25 minutes. Add more water if needed.

4. Serve soup warm.

Nutrition: Calories: 187; Fat: 12g; Phosphorus: 119mg Potassium: 288mg Sodium: 59mg Carbohydrates: 7g Protein: 11g

52. Green Bean Veggie Stew

Preparation Time: 10 minutes
Cooking Time: 30-35 minutes
Serving: 1
Difficulty: Easy
Ingredients:

- 6 cups shredded green cabbage
- 3 celery stalks, chopped
- 1 teaspoon unsalted butter
- ½ large sweet onion, chopped
- 1 teaspoon minced garlic
- 1 scallion, chopped
- 2 tablespoons chopped fresh parsley
- 2 tablespoons lemon juice
- 1 teaspoon chopped fresh oregano
- 1 tablespoon chopped fresh thyme
- 1 teaspoon chopped savory
- 2 cups Water
- 1 cup fresh green beans, cut into 1-inch pieces

- Black pepper (ground), to taste

Directions:

1. Take a medium-large cooking pot, heat butter over medium heat.

2. Add onion and stir-cook until it becomes translucent and soft.

3. Add garlic and stir-cook until it becomes fragrant.

4. Add cabbage, celery, scallion, parsley, lemon juice, thyme, savory, and oregano; add water to cover veggies by 3-4 inches.

5. Stir the mixture and boil it.

6. Over low heat, cover, and simmer the mixture for about 25 minutes until veggies are tender.

7. Add green beans and cook for 2-3 more minutes. Season with black pepper to taste.

8. Serve warm.

Nutrition: Calories: 56; Fat: 1g; Phosphorus: 36mg Potassium: 194mg Sodium: 31mg Carbohydrates: 7g Protein: 1g.

53. Chicken Pasta Soup

Preparation Time: 10 minutes
Cooking Time: 20 minutes
Serving: 1
Difficulty: Easy
Ingredients:

- 1 ½ cups baby spinach
- 2 tablespoons orzo (tiny pasta)
- 1 tablespoon dry white wine
- 1 14-ounce low sodium chicken broth

- 2 plum tomatoes, chopped
- ½ teaspoon Italian seasoning
- 1 large shallot, chopped
- 1 small zucchini, diced
- 8-ounces chicken tenders
- 1 tablespoon extra-virgin olive oil

Directions:

1. Take a medium saucepan or skillet, add oil. Heat over medium heat.

2. Add chicken and stir-cook for 3 minutes until evenly brown. Set aside.

3. In the pan, add zucchini, Italian seasoning, shallot; stir-cook until veggies are softened.

4. Add tomatoes, wine, broth, and orzo.

5. Boil the mixture.

6. Over low heat, cover, and simmer the mixture for about 3 minutes.

7. Mix in spinach and cooked chicken; stir and serve warm.

Nutrition: Calories: 103 Fat: 3g Phosphorus: 125m Potassium: 264mg Sodium: 84mg Carbohydrates: 6g Protein: 12g.

54. Cabbage Turkey Soup

Preparation Time: 10 minutes
Cooking Time: 40-45 minutes
Serving: 1
Difficulty: Easy
Ingredients:

- ½ cup shredded green cabbage
- ½ cup bulgur
- 2 dried bay leaves
- 2 tablespoons chopped fresh parsley
- 1 teaspoon chopped fresh sage

- 1 teaspoon chopped fresh thyme
- 1 celery stalk, chopped
- 1 carrot, sliced thin
- ½ sweet onion, chopped
- 1 teaspoon minced garlic
- 1 teaspoon olive oil
- ½ pound cooked ground turkey, 93% lean
- 4 cups water
- 1 cup chicken stock
- Pinch red pepper flakes
- Black pepper (ground), to taste

Directions:

1. Take a large saucepan or cooking pot, add oil. Heat over medium heat.
2. Add turkey and stir-cook for 4-5 minutes until evenly brown.
3. Add onion and garlic and sauté for about 3 minutes to soften veggies.
4. Add water, chicken stock, cabbage, bulgur, celery, carrot, and bay leaves.
5. Boil the mixture.
6. Over low heat, cover, and simmer the mixture for about 30-35 minutes until bulgur is cooked well and tender.
7. Remove bay leaves. Add parsley, sage, thyme, and red pepper flakes; stir mixture and season with black pepper. Serve warm.

Nutrition: Calories: 83; Fat: 4g; Phosphorus: 91mg Potassium: 185mg Sodium: 63mg Carbohydrates: 2g Protein: 8g.

55. Chicken Fajita Soup

Preparation Time: 10 minutes

Cooking Time: 6 hours 30 minutes
Servings: 2
Stage: 4
Ingredients:
- 2 pounds of boneless skinless chicken breasts
- 1 onion chopped
- 1 green pepper chopped
- 3 garlic cloves minced
- 1 tablespoon butter
- 6 ounces cream cheese
- Salt and pepper to taste

Directions:

Add boneless skinless chicken breasts to a slow cooker and cook for 3 hours on high or 6 hours on low in a cup of chicken broth. Season with salt and pepper.

When the chicken is done, remove from the slow cooker and shred. (You can strain the leftover broth for the soup.)

In a large saucepan fry green pepper, onion, and garlic in 1 tablespoon of butter until they are translucent (2 to 3 minutes). Mash the cream cheese into the veggies with a spoon so that it will combine smoothly as it melts.

Nutrition: Calories: 306kcal Carbohydrates: 8.2g Protein: 26g; Fat: 17g Saturated Fat: 9g Cholesterol: 120mg; Sodium: 880mg Potassium: 757mg Fiber: 1.6g; Sugar: 3g

56. Cream of Chicken Soup

Preparation Time: 10 minutes
Cooking Time: 20 minutes
Servings: 2

Difficulty: Easy

Ingredients:

• 2 cups (500 grams) cauliflower florets

• 2/3 cup (157 ml) unsweetened original almond milk

• 1 cup (250 ml) chicken broth

• 1 teaspoon (5 ml) onion powder

• ½ teaspoon (2.5 ml) grey sea salt

• ¼ teaspoon (1.23 ml) garlic powder

• ¼ teaspoon (1.23 ml) freshly ground black pepper

• 1/8 teaspoon (0.61 ml) celery seed (optional)

• 1/8 teaspoon (0.61 ml) dried thyme

• ¼ cup (30 grams) Beef Gelatin

Directions:

1. Place all ingredients, except cooked chicken and gelatin, in a small saucepan. Cover and bring to a boil over medium heat. Turn heat to low and cook for about 7 to 8 minutes, until cauliflower is softened. Remove from the heat. Add around ½ cup of the hot liquid to a medium-sized bowl using a ladle. Add gelatin, one scoop at a time. Stir until dissolved, then add the next scoop.

2. Serve immediately.

Nutrition: Calories: 198 Calories from Fat: 62.1 Total Fat: 6.9 g Saturated Fat: 1.1 g Cholesterol: 24 mg Sodium: 672 mg Phosphorus: 36m Potassium: 194mg Carbs: 9.4 g Dietary Fiber: 3.8 g Net Carbs: 5.6 g Sugars: 3.3 g Protein: 26.4 g.

57. Beef Stroganoff Soup

Preparation Time: 10 minutes

Cooking Time: 30 minutes

Servings: 4

Difficulty: Easy

Ingredients:

• 2 large beef rump (sirloin) steaks (800 g/ 1.76 lbs.)

• 600 g brown or white mushrooms (1.3 lbs.)

• ¼ cup ghee or lard (55 g/ 1.9 oz.)

• 2 cloves garlic, minced

• 1 medium white or brown onion, chopped (110 g/ 3.9 oz.)

• 5 cups bone broth or chicken stock or vegetable stock (1.2 l/ quart)

• 2 tsps. paprika

• 1 tbsp. of Dijon mustard (you can make your own)

• Juice from 1 lemon (~ 4 tbsp.)

• 1½ cup sour cream or heavy whipping cream (345 g/ 12.2 oz.) - you can use paleo-friendly coconut cream

• ¼ cup freshly chopped parsley

• 1 tsp salt

• ¼ tsp freshly ground black pepper

Directions:

1. Lay the steaks in the freezer in a single layer for 30 to 45 minutes.

2. This will make it easy to slice the steaks into thin strips. Meanwhile, clean and slice the mushrooms.

3. Fry over a medium-high heat until they're cooked through and browned from all sides.

4. Remove the slices from the pan and place them in a bowl. Set aside for later. Do the same for the remaining slices.

5. Grease the pan with the remaining ghee. Add in the chopped onion and minced garlic to the pan and cook until lightly browned and fragrant.

6. Add the sliced mushrooms and cook for 3 to 4 more minutes while stirring occasionally. Then add your Dijon mustard, paprika, and pour in the bone broth. Add lemon juice and boil for 2 to 3 minutes. Add the browned beef slices and sour cream. Remove from heat. If you are using a thickener, add it to the pot and stir well.

7. Finally, add freshly chopped parsley. Eat hot with a slice of toasted Keto Bread or let it cool down and store in the fridge for up to 5 days. Enjoy!

Nutrition: Calories from carbs 7% protein 27%, fat 66 Total carbs 10.8 g Fiber 1.4-gram Sugars 4.8 grams Saturated fat 18.4 grams Sodium 783 mg (34% RDA Potassium 1,398 mg (70% EMR).

58. Paprika Pork Soup

Preparation Time: 5 minutes
Cooking Time: 35 minutes
Servings: 2
Difficulty: Easy
Ingredients:
- 4 oz. sliced pork loin
- 1 tsp. black pepper
- 2 minced garlic cloves
- 1 cup baby spinach
- 3 cups water
- 1 tbsp. extra-virgin olive oil
- 1 chopped onion
- 1 tbsp. paprika

Direction:

1. In a large pot, add the oil, chopped onion and minced garlic.

2. Sauté for 5 minutes on low heat.

3. Add the pork slices to the onions and cook for 7-8 minutes or until browned.

4. Stir in the spinach, reduce heat and simmer for a further 20 minutes or until pork is thoroughly cooked through.

5. Season with pepper to serve.

Nutrition: Calories 165 Protein 13 g Carbs 10 g Fat 9 Sodium (Na) 269 mg Potassium (K) 486 mg Phosphorus 158 mg

59. Green Chicken Enchilada Soup

Preparation Time: 10 minutes
Cooking Time: 5 minutes
Servings: 6
Difficulty: Easy
Ingredients:
- ½ cup salsa Verde
- 4 ounces cream cheese, softened
- 1 cup sharp cheddar cheese, shredded
- 2 cups bone broth or chicken stock
- 2 cups cooked chicken, shredded

Direction:

1. Add the salsa, cream cheese, cheddar cheese and chicken stock in a blender and blend until smooth. Pour into a medium saucepan and cook on medium until hot.

Nutrition: Calories 346 Fat 22 Carbohydrates 3g net Protein 32g

60. Hawaiian Chicken Salad

Preparation Time: 5 minutes
Cooking Time: 30 minutes
Servings: 4
Difficulty: Easy
Ingredients:
- 1 1/2 cups of chicken breast, cooked, chopped
- 1 cup pineapple chunks
- 1 1/4 cups lettuce iceberg, shredded
- 1/2 cup celery, diced
- 1/2 cup mayonnaise
- 1/8 tsp (dash) Tabasco sauce
- 2 lemon juice
- 1/4 tsp black pepper

Directions:
1. Combine the cooked chicken, pineapple, lettuce, and celery in a medium bowl. Just set aside.
2. In a small bowl, make the dressing. Mix the mayonnaise, Tabasco sauce, pepper, and lemon juice.
3. Use the chicken mixture to add the dressing and stir until well mixed.

Nutrition: Power: 310 g, Protein: 16.8 g, Carbohydrates: 9.6 g, fibbers: 1.1 g, Fat: 23.1 g, Sodium: 200 mg, Potassium: 260 mg, Phosphorus: 134 mg

61. Grated Carrot Salad with Lemon-Dijon Vinaigrette

Preparation Time: 15 minutes
Cooking Time: 10 minutes
Servings: 8
Difficulty: Easy
Ingredients:
- 9 small carrots (14 cm), peeled
- 2 tbsp. 1/2 teaspoon Dijon mustard
- 1 C. lemon juice
- 2 tbsp. extra virgin olive oil
- 1-2 tsp. honey (to taste)
- ¼ tsp. Salt
- ¼ tsp. freshly ground pepper (to taste)
- 2 tbsp. chopped parsley
- 1 green onion, thinly sliced

Directions:
1. Grate the carrots in a food processor.
2. Mix Dijon mustard, lemon juice, honey, olive oil, salt, and pepper in a salad bowl. Add the carrots, fresh parsley, and green onions. Stir to coat well. Cover and refrigerate until ready to be served.

Nutrition: Energy: 61 g, Proteins: 1 g, Carbohydrates: 7 g, fibbers: 1 g, Total Fat: 4 g, Sodium: 88 mg, Phosphorus: 22 mg, Potassium: 197 mg

62. Tuna Macaroni Salad

Preparation Time: 5 minutes
Cooking Time: 25 minutes
Servings: 10
Difficulty: Easy
Ingredients:
- 1 1/2 cups Uncooked Macaroni
- 1 170g Can of tuna in water
- 1/4 cup Mayonnaise
- 2 medium celery stalks, diced
- 1 Tbsp. Lemon Pepper Seasoning

Directions:

1.   Cook the pasta and let it cool in the refrigerator.

2.   Drain the tuna in a colander and rinse it with cold water.

3.   Add the tuna and celery once the macaroni has cooled.

4.   Stir in mayonnaise and sprinkle with lemon seasoning. Mix well. Serve cold.

Nutrition: Power: 136 g, Protein: 8.0 g, Carbohydrates: 18 g, fibbers: 0.8 g, Fat: 3.6 g, Sodium: 75 mg, Potassium: 124 mg, Phosphorus: 90 mg

63.   Couscous Salad

Preparation Time: 5 minutes
Cooking Time: 5 minutes
Servings: 5
Difficulty: Easy
Ingredients:

*   3 cups of water
*   1/2 tsp. cinnamon tea
*   1/2 tsp. cumin tea
*   1 tsp. honey soup
*   2 tbsp. lemon juice
*   3 cups quick-cooking couscous
*   2 tbsp. tea of olive oil
*   1 green onion,
*   Finely chopped 1 small carrot, finely diced
*   1/2 red pepper,
*   Finely diced fresh coriander

Directions:

Stir in the water with the cinnamon, cumin, honey, and lemon juice and bring to a boil. Put the couscous in it, cover it, and remove it from the heat.

To swell the couscous, stir with a fork. Add the vegetables, fresh herbs, and olive oil. It is possible to serve the salad warm or cold.

Nutrition: Energy: 190 g, Protein: 6 g, Carbohydrates: 38 g, fibbers: 2 g, Total Fat: 1 g, Sodium: 4 mg, Phosphorus: 82 mg, Potassium: 116 mg

64.   Fruity Zucchini Salad

Preparation Time: 5 minutes
Cooking Time: 5 minutes
Servings: 4
Difficulty: Easy
Ingredients:

*   400g zucchini
*   1 small onion
*   4 tbsp. olive oil
*   100g pineapple preserve, drained
*   Salt, paprika to taste
*   Thyme to taste

Directions:

1.   Dice the onions and sauté in the oil until translucent.

2.   Cut the zucchini into slices and add—season with salt, paprika, and thyme.

3.   Let cool and mix with the cut pineapple.

Nutrition: Energy: 150kcal, Protein: 2g, Fat: 10g, Carbohydrates: 10g, Dietary fibbers: 2g, Potassium: 220mg, Calcium: 38mg, Sodium 24mg Phosphorus: 213 mg

65.   Cucumber Salad, Pulled Through Slowly

Preparation Time: 5 minutes

Cooking Time: 5 minutes
Servings: 4
Difficulty: medium
Ingredients:
- 1 cucumber
- 1 tbsp. salt
- 100 ml of water
- 100 ml white wine vinegar
- 2 tbsp. cane sugar
- 5 peppercorns, crushed
- 1/2 teaspoon cinnamon
- 1/2 teaspoon of allspice
- 1 teaspoon chili powder
- 1 teaspoon ginger powder

Directions:
1. Wash the cucumber, cut it into thin slices, put them in a bowl, sprinkle with salt, and stir, shake well so that the salt gets everywhere. Then let it steep for half an hour.
2. Meanwhile, in a saucepan, mix water, vinegar, sugar, pepper, cinnamon, allspice, chili, ginger, and bring to a boil once, then let cool again with the lid closed.
3. Rinse the lettuce slices and pour off the water. If necessary, dry in a towel. Add the pot's dressing to the salad slices and let everything sit in the fridge for a day.

Nutrition: Energy: 49kcal, Protein: 1g, Carbohydrates: 5g, Potassium: 234mg, Sodium: 500mg, Calcium: 34mg, Phosphate: 21mg Phosphorus: 142 mg

66. Tortellini Salad

Preparation Time: 5 minutes
Cooking Time: 10 minutes

Servings: 4
Difficulty: medium
Ingredients:
- 200g tortellini with meat filling
- 100g red peppers
- 1 tomato
- 1 clove of garlic
- Salt pepper
- Fresh basil, some leaves
- 3 tbsp. rapeseed oil
- 1 tbsp. white wine vinegar

Directions:
1. Cook the tortellini in salted water according to the instructions on the packet and drain.
2. Finely dice the pepper and garlic and sweat in the rapeseed oil. Add the vinegar and spices and pour over the tortellini. Cut the tomato into small pieces and mix in. mix with the fresh basil and season to taste.

Nutrition: Energy: 161kcal, Protein: 4g, Fat: 9g, Carbohydrates: 18g, Dietary fibbers: 3g, Potassium: 173mg, Phosphorus: 95 mg Sodium: 36mg, Phosphate: 80mg

67. Farmer's Salad

Preparation Time: 5 minutes
Cooking Time: 5 minutes
Servings: 2
Difficulty: medium
Ingredients:
- 60g mixed leaf salads
- 100g red pepper, diced
- 200g green beans
- 60g feta cheese
- 1 tbsp. wine vinegar

- 1 tbsp. diced onions
- Salt, pepper, sugar
- 2 tbsp. olive oil

Directions:

1. Mix vinegar with onions, oil, and spices and mix with the salad.

2. Cut the sheep's cheese into cubes and serve with the salad. It goes well with a baguette or flatbread with herb butter.

Nutrition: Energy: 187kcal, Protein: 8g, Fat: 16g, Carbohydrates: 4g, Dietary fibers: 5g, Potassium: 396mg, Phosphorus: 288 mg Sodium: 231mg, Calcium: 188mg, Phosphate: 170mg

68. Chicken and Asparagus Salad with Watercress

Preparation Time: 5 minutes
Cooking Time: 40 minutes
Servings: 4
Difficulty: medium
Ingredients:

- 100 g spring onions (0.5 bunch)
- 100 g green asparagus
- 600 g chicken breast fillet (4 chicken breast fillets)
- salt to taste
- pepper to taste
- 1 small lime
- 1 clove of garlic
- 6 tbsp. honey
- 1 tbsp. grainy mustard
- 5 tbsp. olive oil
- 100 g watercress

Directions:

1. The spring onions are cleaned and washed and then cut into thin rings.

2. The woody ends of the asparagus are cut off. Wash and pat the asparagus to dry. Halve the sticks and, with a peeler, cut the halves lengthwise into thin slices.

3. Wash the fillets of chicken, pat them dry with kitchen paper, and cut them into strips. With salt and pepper, season.

4. Trim the lime in half for the dressing and squeeze out the juice. Peel the garlic and dice it. Mix the mustard, 3 tablespoons of lime juice, and 3 tablespoons of oil with the honey. With salt and pepper, season.

5. Heat the remaining oil in a large non-stick pan and stir-fry the meat over high heat for about 5 minutes.

6. In a bowl, add the chicken, spring onions, and asparagus. Mix in the dressing and allow the salad too steep for 10 minutes or so.

7. Meanwhile, wash the cress and shake it dry. Pluck the leaves, chop coarsely as desired, and spread on dishes or bowls. Use salt and pepper to season the chicken salad and serve on the cress.

Nutrition: Calories 368 kcal (18%), Protein 37 g (38%), Fat 14 g (12%), Carbohydrates 22 g (15%), added sugar 17 g (68%), fibbers 2 g (7%) Phosphorous 168mg, Potassium 241mg Sodium: 163 mg

69. Cucumber Salad

Preparation Time: 5 minutes
Cooking Time: 5 minutes
Servings: 4

Difficulty: medium
Ingredients:
- 1 tbsp. dried dill
- 1 onion
- ¼ cup water
- 1 cup vinegar
- 3 cucumbers
- ¾ cup white sugar

Direction:
1. In a bowl, add all ingredients and mix well
2. Serve with dressing

Nutrition: Calories 49, Fat 0.1g, Sodium (Na) 341mg, Potassium (K) 171mg, Protein 0.8g, Carbs 11g, Phosphorus 24 mg

70. Broccoli-Cauliflower Salad

Preparation Time: 5 minutes
Cooking Time: 5 minutes
Servings: 4
Difficulty: medium
Ingredients:
- 1 tbsp. wine vinegar
- 1 cup cauliflower florets
- ¼ cup white sugar
- 2 cups hard-cooked eggs
- 5 slices bacon
- 1 cup broccoli florets
- 1 cup cheddar cheese
- 1 cup mayonnaise

Direction:
1. In a bowl, add all ingredients and mix well
2. Serve with dressing

Nutrition: Calories 89.8, Fat 4.5 g, Sodium (Na) 51.2 mg, Potassium (K) 257.6 mg, Carbs 11.5 g, Protein 3.0 g, Phosphorus 47 mg

71. Macaroni Salad

Preparation Time: 5 minutes
Cooking Time: 5 minutes
Servings: 4
Difficulty: medium
Ingredients:
- ¼ tsp. celery seed
- 2 hard-boiled eggs
- 2 cups salad dressing
- 1 onion
- 2 tsp. white vinegar
- 2 stalks celery
- 2 cups cooked macaroni
- 1 red bell pepper
- 2 tbsps. mustard

Direction:
1. In a bowl, add all ingredients and mix well
2. Serve with dressing

Nutrition: Calories 360, Fat 21g, Sodium (Na) 400mg, Carbs 36g, Protein 6g, Potassium (K) 68mg, Phosphorus 36 mg

72. Pear & Brie Salad

Preparation Time: 5 minutes
Cooking Time: 0 minutes
Servings: 4
Difficulty: medium
Ingredients:
- 1 tablespoon olive oil
- 1 cup arugula

- ½ lemon
- ½ cup canned pears
- ¼ cucumber
- ¼ cup chopped brie

Direction:
1. Peel and dice the cucumber.
2. Dice the pear.
3. Wash the arugula.
4. Combine salad in a serving bowl and crumble the brie over the top.
5. Whisk the olive oil and lemon juice together.
6. Drizzle over the salad.
7. Season with a bit of black pepper to taste and serve immediately.

Nutrition: Calories 54, Protein 1 g, Carbs 12 g, Fat 7 g, Sodium 57mg, Potassium 115 mg, Phosphorus 67 mg

73. Creamy Tuna Salad

Preparation Time: 10 minutes
Cooking Time: 5 minutes
Servings: 4
Difficulty: medium
Ingredients:
- 3.5 oz. can tuna, drained and flaked
- 1 1/2 tsp garlic powder
- 1 tbsp. dill, chopped
- 1 tsp curry powder
- 2 tbsp. fresh lemon juice
- 1/2 cup onion, chopped
- 1/2 cup celery, chopped
- 1/4 cup parmesan cheese, grated
- 3/4 cup mayonnaise

Directions:

1. Add all ingredients into the large bowl and mix until well combined.
2. Serve and enjoy.

Nutrition: Calories 224 Fat 15.5 g Carbohydrates 14.1 g Sugar 4.2 g Protein 8 g Cholesterol 20 mg Phosphorus: 110mg Potassium: 117mg Sodium: 75mg

74. Caesar Salad

Preparation Time: 5 minutes
Cooking Time: 5 minutes
Servings: 4
Difficulty: medium
Ingredients:
- 1 head romaine lettuce
- ¼ cup mayonnaise
- 1 tablespoon lemon juice
- 4 anchovy fillets
- 1 teaspoon Worcestershire sauce
- Black pepper
- 5 garlic cloves
- 4 tablespoons. Parmesan cheese
- 1 teaspoon mustard

Direction:
1. In a bowl mix all ingredients and mix well
2. Serve with dressing

Nutrition: Calories 44, Fat 2.1 g, Sodium 83 mg, Potassium 216 mg, Carbs 4.3 g, Protein 3.2 g, Phosphorus 45.6mg Calcium 19mg, Potassium 27mg Sodium: 121 mg

75. Thai Cucumber Salad

Preparation Time: 5 minutes
Cooking Time: 5 minutes
Servings: 2

Difficulty: medium

Ingredients:

- ¼ cup chopped peanuts
- ¼ cup white sugar
- ½ cup cilantro
- ¼ cup rice wine vinegar
- 3 cucumbers
- 2 jalapeno peppers

Direction:

1. Add all ingredients in a small basin and combine well
2. Serve with dressing

Nutrition: Calories 20, Fat 0g, Sodium 85mg, Carbs 5g, Protein 1g, Potassium 190.4 mg, Phosphorus 46.8mg

76. Barb's Asian Slaw

Preparation Time: 5 minutes
Cooking Time: 5 minutes
Servings: 2
Difficulty: medium
Ingredients:

- 1 cabbage head, shredded
- 4 chopped green onions
- ½ cup slivered or sliced almonds

Dressing:

- ½ cup olive oil
- ¼ cup tamari or soy sauce
- 1 tablespoon honey or maple syrup
- 1 tablespoon baking stevia

Directions:

1. Heat dressing **ingredients** in a saucepan on the stove until thoroughly mixed.
2. Mix all ingredients when you are ready to serve.

Nutrition: Calories: 205 Protein: 27g Carbohydrate: 12g Fat: 10 g Calcium 29mg, Phosphorous 76mg, Potassium 27mg Sodium: 111 mg

77. Green Bean and Potato Salad

Preparation Time: 5 minutes
Cooking Time: 5 minutes
Servings: 4
Difficulty: medium
Ingredients:

- ½ cup basil
- ¼ cup olive oil
- 1 tablespoon mustard
- ¾ lb. green beans
- 1 tablespoon lemon juice
- ½ cup balsamic vinegar
- 1 red onion
- 1 lb. red carrots
- 1 garlic clove

Direction:

1. Place carrots in a pot with water and bring to a boil for 15-18 minutes or until tender
2. Thrown in green beans after 5-6 minutes
3. Drain and cut into cubes
4. In a bowl, add all ingredients and mix well
5. Serve with dressing

Nutrition: Calories 153.2, Fat 2.0 g, Sodium 77.6 mg, Potassium 759.0 mg, Carbs 29.0 g, Protein 6.9 g, Phosphorus 49 mg

78. Italian Cucumber Salad

Preparation Time: 5 minutes
Cooking Time: 0 minutes
Servings: 2
Difficulty: medium
Ingredients:
- 1/4 cup rice vinegar
- 1/8 teaspoon stevia
- 1/2 teaspoon olive oil
- 1/8 teaspoon black pepper
- 1/2 cucumber, sliced
- 1 cup carrots, sliced
- 2 tablespoons green onion, sliced
- 2 tablespoons red bell pepper, sliced
- 1/2 teaspoon Italian seasoning blend

Direction:
1.   Put all the salad **ingredients** into a suitable salad bowl.
2.   Toss them well and refrigerate for 1 hour.
3.   Serve.
Nutrition: Calories 112 Total Fat 1.6g Cholesterol 0mg Sodium 43mg Protein 2.3g Phosphorous 198mg Potassium 529mg

79. Grapes Jicama Salad

Preparation Time: 5 minutes
Cooking Time: 0 minutes
Servings: 2
Difficulty: medium
Ingredients:
- 1 jicama, peeled and sliced
- 1 carrot, sliced
- 1/2 medium red onion, sliced
- 1 ¼ cup seedless grapes
- 1/3 cup fresh basil leaves
- 1 tablespoon apple cider vinegar
- 1 ½ tablespoon lemon juice
- 1 ½ tablespoon lime juice

Direction:
1.   Put all the salad **ingredients** into a suitable salad bowl.
2.   Toss them well and refrigerate for 1 hour.
3.   Serve.
Nutrition: Calories 203 Total Fat 0.7g Sodium 44mg Protein 3.7g Calcium 79mg Phosphorous 141mg Potassium 429mg

80. Cucumber Couscous Salad

Preparation Time: 5 minutes
Cooking Time: 0 minutes
Servings: 4
Difficulty: medium
Ingredients:
- 1 cucumber, sliced
- ½ cup red bell pepper, sliced
- ¼ cup sweet onion, sliced
- ¼ cup parsley, chopped
- ½ cup couscous, cooked
- 2 tablespoons olive oil
- 2 tablespoons rice vinegar
- 2 tablespoons feta cheese crumbled
- 1 ½ teaspoon dried basil
- 1/4 teaspoon black pepper

Direction:
1.   Put all the salad **ingredients** into a suitable salad bowl.
2.   Toss them well and refrigerate for 1 hour.

3.   Serve.

Nutrition: Calories 202 Total Fat 9.8g Sodium 258mg Protein 6.2g Calcium 80mg Phosphorous 192mg Potassium 209mg

DINNER

81. Spring Vegetable Soup

Preparation time: 10 minutes
Cooking time: 45 minutes
Servings: 4
Difficulty: easy
INGREDIENTS
- 1 cup fresh green beans, chopped
- ¾ cup celery, chopped
- ½ cup onion, chopped
- ½ cup carrots, chopped
- ½ cup mushrooms, chopped
- ½ cup frozen corn
- 1 medium Roma tomato, chopped
- 2 tablespoons olive oil
- ½ cup frozen corn
- 4 cups vegetable broth
- 1 teaspoon dried oregano leaves
- 1 teaspoon garlic powder

DIRECTIONS
1. Place a suitably-sized cooking pot over medium heat and add olive oil to heat.
2. Toss in onion and celery, then sauté until soft.
3. Stir in the corn and rest of the ingredients and cook the soup to boil.
4. Now reduce its heat to a simmer and cook for 45 minutes.
5. Serve warm.

NUTRITION: Calories: 114 Protein: 2 g Carbohydrates: 13 g Fat: 6 g Cholesterol: 0 mg Sodium: 262 mg Potassium: 400 mg Phosphorus: 108 mg Calcium: 48 mg Fiber: 3.4 g

82. Seafood Corn Chowder

Preparation time: 10 minutes
Cooking time: 12 minutes
Servings: 4
Difficulty: easy
INGREDIENTS
- 1 tablespoon butter
- 1 cup onion, chopped
- 1/3 cup celery, chopped
- ½ cup green bell pepper, chopped
- ½ cup red bell pepper, chopped
- 1 tablespoon white flour
- 14 ounces chicken broth
- 2 cups cream
- 6 ounces evaporated milk
- 10 ounces surimi imitation crab chunks
- 2 cups frozen corn kernels
- ½ teaspoon black pepper
- ½ teaspoon paprika

DIRECTIONS
1. Place a suitably-sized saucepan over medium heat and add butter to melt.
2. Toss in onion, green and red peppers, and celery, then sauté for 5 minutes.
3. Stir in flour and whisk well for 2 minutes.

4. Pour in chicken broth and stir until it boils.
5. Add evaporated milk, corn, surimi crab, paprika, black pepper, and creamer.
6. Cook for 5 minutes then serve warm.

NUTRITION: Calories: 173 Protein: 8 g Carbohydrates: 22 g Fat: 7 g Cholesterol: 13 mg Sodium: 160 mg Potassium: 285 mg Phosphorus: 181 mg Calcium: 68 mg Fiber: 1.5 g

83. Beef Sage Soup

Preparation time: 10 minutes
Cooking time: 20 minutes
Servings: 4
Difficulty: easy
INGREDIENTS
- ½ pound ground beef
- ½ teaspoon ground sage
- ½ teaspoon black pepper
- ½ teaspoon dried basil
- ½ teaspoon garlic powder
- 4 slices bread, cubed
- 2 tablespoons olive oil
- 1 tablespoon herb seasoning blend
- 2 garlic cloves, minced
- 3 cups chicken broth
- 1 ½ cups water
- 4 tablespoons fresh parsley
- 2 tablespoons parmesan cheese, grated

DIRECTIONS
1. Preheat your oven to 375ºF.
2. Mix beef with sage, basil, black pepper, and garlic powder in a bowl, then set it aside.
3. Toss the bread cubes with olive oil in a baking sheet and bake them for 8 minutes.
4. Meanwhile, sauté the beef mixture in a greased cooking pot until it is browned.
5. Stir in garlic and sauté for 2 minutes, then add parsley, water, and broth.
6. Cover the beef soup and cook for 10 minutes on a simmer.
7. Garnish the soup with parmesan cheese and baked bread.
8. Serve warm.

NUTRITION: Calories: 335 Protein: 26 g Carbohydrates: 15 g Fat: 19 g Cholesterol: 250 mg Sodium: 374 mg Potassium: 392 mg Phosphorus: 268 mg Calcium: 118 mg Fiber: 0.9 g

84. Cabbage Borscht

Preparation time: 10 minutes
Cooking time: 1 hour, 30 minutes
Servings: 6
Difficulty: easy
INGREDIENTS
- 2 pounds beef steaks
- 6 cups cold water
- 2 tablespoons olive oil
- ½ cup tomato sauce
- 1 medium cabbage, chopped
- 1 cup onion, diced
- 1 cup carrots, diced
- 1 cup turnips, peeled and diced

- 1 teaspoon pepper
- 6 tablespoons lemon juice
- 4 tablespoons sugar

DIRECTIONS

1. Start by placing steak in a large cooking pot and pour enough water to cover it.
2. Cover the beef pot and cook it on a simmer until it is tender, then shred it using a fork.
3. Add olive oil, onion, tomato sauce, carrots, turnips, and shredded steak to the cooking liquid in the pot.
4. Stir in black pepper, sugar, and lemon juice to season the soup.
5. Cover the cabbage soup and cook on low heat for 1 ½ hour.
6. Serve warm.

NUTRITION: Calories: 202 Protein: 19 g Carbohydrates: 9 g Fat: 10 g Cholesterol: 60 mg Sodium: 242 mg Potassium: 388 mg Phosphorus: 160 mg Calcium: 46 mg Fiber: 2.1 g

85. Ground Beef Soup

Preparation time: 10 minutes
Cooking time: 30 minutes
Servings: 4
Difficulty: easy
INGREDIENTS

- 1-pound lean ground beef
- ½ cup onion, chopped
- 2 teaspoons lemon-pepper seasoning blend
- 1 cup beef broth
- 2 cups of water

- 1/3 cup white rice, uncooked
- 3 cups frozen mixed vegetables
- 1 tablespoon sour cream

DIRECTIONS

1. Spray a saucepan with cooking oil and place it over medium heat.
2. Toss in onion and ground beef, then sauté until brown.
3. Stir in broth and rest of the ingredients, then boil it.
4. Reduce heat to a simmer, then cover the soup to cook for 30 minutes.
5. Garnish with sour cream.
6. Enjoy.

NUTRITION: Calories: 222 Protein: 20 g Carbohydrates: 19 g Fat: 8 g Cholesterol: 52 mg Sodium: 170 mg Potassium: 448 mg Phosphorus: 210 mg Calcium: 43 mg Fiber: 4.3 g

86. Shrimp and Crab Gumbo

Preparation time: 10 minutes
Cooking time: 15 minutes
Servings: 4
Difficulty: easy
INGREDIENTS

- 1 cup bell pepper, chopped
- 1 ½ cups onion, chopped
- 1 garlic clove, chopped
- ¼ cup celery leaves, chopped
- 1 cup green onion tops
- ¼ cup fresh parsley, chopped
- 4 tablespoons canola oil
- 6 tablespoons all-purpose white flour

- 3 cups of water
- 4 cups chicken broth
- 8 ounces shrimp, uncooked
- 6 ounces crab meat
- ¼ teaspoon black pepper
- 1 teaspoon hot sauce
- 3 cups cooked rice

DIRECTIONS

1. Prepare the roux in a suitably-sized pan by heating oil in it.
2. Stir in flour and sauté until it changes its color.
3. Pour in 1 cup water, then add onion, garlic, celery leaves, and bell pepper.
4. Cover the roux mixture and cook on low heat until the veggies turn soft.
5. Add 2 cups water and 4 cups broth, then mix again.
6. Continue cooking it for 5 minutes then add crab meat and shrimp.
7. Cook for 10 minutes then and parsley and green onion.
8. Continue cooking for 5 minutes then garnish with black pepper and hot sauce.
9. Serve warm with rice.

NUTRITION: Calories: 327 Protein: 22 g Carbohydrates: 33 g Fat: 11 g Cholesterol: 86 mg Sodium: 328 mg Potassium: 368 mg Phosphorus: 221 mg Calcium: 79 mg Fiber: 1.4 g

87. Tangy Turkey Soup

Preparation time: 10 minutes
Cooking time: 68 minutes
Servings: 4

Difficulty: easy

INGREDIENTS

- 1 cup carrots, chopped
- 1 cup celery, chopped
- 1 cup green bell pepper, chopped
- 1 cup yellow onion, chopped
- ½ cup fresh tomato, chopped
- ½ cup fresh parsley, chopped
- 2 garlic cloves, chopped
- 1 cup mushrooms, sliced
- 2 cups zucchini, sliced
- 1 tablespoon olive oil
- 1-pound turkey breast, skinless, cubed
- ½ teaspoon black pepper
- ½ cup dry white wine
- 4 cups chicken broth
- 1 teaspoon dried thyme
- 1 bay leaf
- ¼ teaspoon crushed red pepper
- 3 cups white rice, cooked
- 3 tablespoons lemon juice

DIRECTIONS

1. Place a suitably-sized stockpot over medium heat and oil to heat.
2. Toss in turkey, and black pepper, then sauté for 10 minutes.
3. Stir in green bell pepper, onion, celery, and carrots, then sauté for 8 minutes.
4. Add garlic, tomato, and wine then cook for 2 minutes.
5. Stir in bay leaf, thyme, broth, and red pepper then cook for 30 minutes on a simmer.

6. Add zucchini, mushrooms, parsley, and rice to the soup then continue cooking for 15 minutes.
7. Serve warm with lemon juice on top.

NUTRITION: Calories: 214 Protein: 18 g Carbohydrates: 22 g Fat: 6 g Cholesterol: 24 mg Sodium: 128 mg Potassium: 528 mg Phosphorus: 197 mg Calcium: 54 mg Fiber: 2.4 g

88. Spaghetti Squash & Yellow Bell-Pepper Soup

Preparation time: 10 minutes
Cooking time: 45 minutes
Servings: 4
Difficulty: easy
INGREDIENTS

- 2 diced yellow bell peppers
- 2 chopped large garlic cloves
- 1 peeled and cubed spaghetti squash
- 1 quartered and sliced onion
- 1 tablespoon dried thyme
- 1 tablespoon coconut oil
- 1 teaspoon curry powder
- 4 cups water

DIRECTIONS

1. Heat the oil in a large pan over medium-high heat before sweating the onions and garlic for 3-4 minutes.
2. Sprinkle over the curry powder.
3. Add the stock and bring to a boil over a high heat before adding the squash, pepper and thyme.
4. Turn down the heat, cover and allow to simmer for 25-30 minutes.

5. Continue to simmer until squash is soft if needed.
6. Allow to cool before blitzing in a blender/food processor until smooth.
7. Serve!

NUTRITION: Calories 103, Protein 2 g, Carbs 17 g, Fat 4 g, Sodium (Na) 32 mg, Potassium (K)365 mg, Phosphorus 50 mg

89. Red Pepper & Brie Soup

Preparation time: 10 minutes
Cooking time: 35 minutes
Servings: 4
Difficulty: easy
INGREDIENTS

- 1 teaspoon paprika
- 1 teaspoon cumin
- 1 chopped red onion
- 2 chopped garlic cloves
- ¼ cup crumbled brie
- 2 tablespoons. extra virgin olive oil
- 4 chopped red bell peppers
- 4 cups water

DIRECTIONS

1. Heat the oil in a pot over medium heat.
2. Sweat the onions and peppers for 5 minutes.
3. Add the garlic cloves, cumin and paprika and sauté for 3-4 minutes.
4. Add the water and allow to boil before turning the heat down to simmer for 30 minutes.

5. Remove from the heat and allow to cool slightly.
6. Put the mixture in a food processor and blend until smooth.
7. Pour into serving bowls and add the crumbled brie to the top with a little black pepper.
8. Enjoy!

NUTRITION: Calories 152, Protein 3 g, Carbs 8 g, Fat 11 g, Sodium (Na) 66 mg, Potassium (K) 270 mg, Phosphorus 207 mg

90. Turkey & Lemon-Grass Soup

Preparation time: 5 minutes
Cooking time: 40 minutes
Servings: 4
Difficulty: easy
INGREDIENTS

- 1 fresh lime
- ¼ cup fresh basil leaves
- 1 tablespoon cilantro
- 1 cup canned and drained water chestnuts
- 1 tablespoon coconut oil
- 1 thumb-size minced ginger piece
- 2 chopped scallions
- 1 finely chopped green chili
- 4ounce skinless and sliced turkey breasts
- 1 minced garlic clove, minced
- ½ finely sliced stick lemon-grass
- 1 chopped white onion, chopped
- 4 cups water

DIRECTIONS

1. Crush the lemon-grass, cilantro, chili, 1 tablespoon oil and basil leaves in a blender or pestle and mortar to form a paste.
2. Heat a large pan/wok with 1 tablespoon olive oil on high heat.
3. Sauté the onions, garlic and ginger until soft.
4. Add the turkey and brown each side for 4-5 minutes.
5. Add the broth and stir.
6. Now add the paste and stir.
7. Next add the water chestnuts, turn down the heat slightly and allow to simmer for 25-30 minutes or until turkey is thoroughly cooked through.
8. Serve hot with the green onion sprinkled over the top.

NUTRITION: Calories 123, Protein 10 g, Carbs 12 g, Fat 3 g, Sodium (Na) 501 mg, Potassium (K) 151 mg, Phosphorus 110 mg

91. Curried Fish Cakes

Preparation Time: 10 minutes
Cooking Time: 18 minutes
Servings: 4
Difficulty: easy
INGREDIENTS

- ¾ pound Atlantic cod, cubed
- 1 apple, peeled and cubed

- 1 tablespoon yellow curry paste
- 2 tablespoons cornstarch
- 1 tablespoon peeled grated ginger root
- 1 large egg
- 1 tablespoon freshly squeezed lemon juice
- ⅛ teaspoon freshly ground black pepper
- ½ cup crushed puffed rice cereal
- 1 tablespoon olive oil

DIRECTIONS

1. Put the cod, apple, curry, cornstarch, ginger, egg, lemon juice, and pepper in a blender or food processor and process until finely chopped. Avoid over-processing, or the mixture will become mushy.
2. Place the rice cereal on a shallow plate.
3. Form the mixture into 8 patties.
4. Dredge the patties in the rice cereal to coat.
5. Heat the oil in a large skillet over medium heat.
6. Cook patties for 4 to 5 minutes per side, turning once until a meat thermometer registers 160°F.
7. Serve.

NUTRITION: Per Serving: Calories: 188; Total fat: 6g; Saturated fat: 1g; Sodium: 150mg; Potassium: 292mg; Phosphorus: 150mg; Carbohydrates: 12g; Fiber: 1g; Protein: 21g; Sugar: 5g

92. Shrimp Fettuccine

Preparation Time: 20 minutes
Cooking Time: 10 minutes
Servings: 6
Difficulty: easy

INGREDIENTS

- 2 tablespoons olive oil
- 1 leek, white and green parts, chopped
- 12 ounces whole-wheat fettuccine pasta
- 1 cup green beans, cut into 1-inch pieces
- 1 red bell pepper, chopped
- ½ pound medium raw shrimp, peeled and deveined
- 1 cup low-sodium vegetable broth
- ½ teaspoon dried thyme leaves
- 2 tablespoons chopped fresh chives
- 3 tablespoons grated Parmesan cheese

DIRECTIONS

1. Bring a large pot of water to a boil.
2. Meanwhile, heat the olive oil in a large skillet over medium heat.
3. Sauté the leek for 2 minutes.
4. Add the pasta to the boiling water; cook according to package instructions, until the fettuccine is al dente.

5. Add the green beans and red bell pepper to the skillet and sauté for 2 minutes.
6. Add the shrimp to the skillet and sauté for 1 minute.
7. Drain the pasta, reserving ½ cup cooking water.
8. Add the pasta, broth, and thyme to the skillet and cook for 3 to 4 minutes or until the sauce reduces slightly and the shrimp curls and turns pink.
9. Sprinkle with the chives and cheese and serve.

NUTRITION: Per Serving: Calories: 310; Total fat: 6g; Saturated fat: 1g; Sodium: 130mg; Potassium: 340mg; Phosphorus: 274mg; Carbohydrates: 48g; Fiber: 6g; Protein: 19g; Sugar: 2g

93. Baked Sole with Caramelized Onion

Preparation Time: 10 minutes
Cooking Time: 20 minutes
Servings: 4
Difficulty: easy
INGREDIENTS
- 1 cup finely chopped onion
- ½ cup low-sodium vegetable broth
- 1 yellow summer squash, sliced
- 2 cups frozen broccoli florets
- 4 (3-ounce) fillets of sole
- Pinch salt
- 2 tablespoons olive oil
- Pinch baking soda
- 2 teaspoons avocado oil
- 1 teaspoon dried basil leaves

DIRECTIONS
1. Preheat the oven to 425°F.
2. In a medium skillet over medium-high heat, add the onions. Cook for 1 minute; then, stirring constantly, cook for another 4 minutes.
3. Remove the onions from the heat.
4. Pour the broth into a baking sheet with a lip and arrange the squash and broccoli on the sheet in a single layer. Top the vegetables with the fish. Sprinkle the fish with the salt and drizzle everything with the olive oil.
5. Bake the fish and the vegetables for 10 minutes.
6. While the fish is baking, return the skillet with the onions to medium-high heat and stir in a pinch of baking soda. Stir in the avocado oil and cook for 5 minutes, stirring frequently, until the onions are dark brown.
7. Transfer the onions to a plate.
8. Remove the baking sheet from the oven and top the fish evenly with the onions. Sprinkle with the basil.
9. Return the fish to the oven and bake 8 to10 minutes longer or until the fish flakes when tested with a fork and the vegetables are tender. Serve the fish on the vegetables.

NUTRITION: Per Serving: Calories: 200; Total fat: 11g; Saturated fat: 2g; Sodium: 320mg; Potassium: 537; Phosphorus: 331mg; Carbohydrates: 10g; Fiber: 3g; Protein: 16g; Sugar: 4g

94. Veggie Seafood Stir-Fry

Preparation Time: 12 minutes
Cooking Time: 18 minutes
Servings: 6
Difficulty: easy
INGREDIENTS

- 1 cup low-sodium vegetable or chicken broth
- 1 tablespoon cornstarch
- ½ teaspoon ground ginger
- ⅛ teaspoon red pepper flakes
- 2 tablespoons olive oil
- 1 onion, chopped
- 2 carrots, peeled and thinly sliced
- 1-pound medium raw shrimp, peeled and deveined
- 1 cup snow peas
- 2 tablespoons sesame oil
- 2 cups cooked brown rice

DIRECTIONS

1. In a small bowl, combine the broth, cornstarch, ginger, and red pepper flakes and set aside.
2. Heat the oil in a wok or large skillet over medium-high heat.
3. Stir-fry the onion and carrots for 3 to 4 minutes until tender-crisp.
4. Add the shrimp and snow peas and stir-fry for 3 minutes longer or until the shrimp curl and turn pink.

5. Add the sauce and stir-fry for 1 to 2 minutes longer or until the sauce bubbles and thickens.
6. Drizzle with the sesame oil and serve over the rice.

NUTRITION: Per Serving: Calories: 306; Total fat: 15g; Saturated fat: 2g; Sodium: 127mg; Potassium: 385mg; Phosphorus: 269mg; Carbohydrates: 24g; Fiber: 2g; Protein: 21g; Sugar: 3g

95. Thai Tuna Wraps

Preparation Time: 10 minutes
Cooking Time: 0 minute
Servings: 4
Difficulty: easy
INGREDIENTS

- ¼ cup unsalted peanut butter
- 2 tablespoons freshly squeezed lemon juice
- 1 teaspoon low-sodium soy sauce
- ½ teaspoon ground ginger
- ⅛ teaspoon cayenne pepper
- 1 (6-ounce) can no-salt-added or low-sodium chunk light tuna, drained
- 1 cup shredded red cabbage
- 2 scallions, white and green parts, chopped
- 1 cup grated carrots
- 8 butter lettuce leaves

DIRECTIONS

1. In a medium bowl, stir together the peanut butter, lemon juice, soy sauce, ginger, and cayenne pepper until well combined.

2. Stir in the tuna, cabbage, scallions, and carrots.
3. Divide the tuna filling evenly between the butter lettuce leaves and serve.

NUTRITION: Per Serving: Calories: 172; Total fat; 9g; Saturated fat: 1g; Sodium: 98mg; Potassium: 421mg; Phosphorus: 153mg; Carbohydrates: 8g; Fiber: 2g; Protein: 17g; Sugar: 4g

96. Grilled Fish and Vegetable Packets

Preparation Time: 15 minutes
Cooking Time: 12 minutes
Servings: 4
Difficulty: easy
INGREDIENTS

- 1 (8-ounce) package sliced mushrooms
- 1 leek, white and green parts, chopped
- 1 cup frozen corn
- 4 (4-ounce) Atlantic cod fillets
- Juice of 1 lemon
- 3 tablespoons olive oil

DIRECTIONS

1. Prepare and preheat the grill to medium coals and set a grill 6 inches from the coals.
2. Tear off four 30-inch long strips of heavy-duty aluminum foil.
3. Arrange the mushrooms, leek, and corn in the center of each piece of foil and top with the fish.
4. Drizzle the packet contents evenly with the lemon juice and olive oil.
5. Bring the longer length sides of the foil together at the top and, holding the edges together, fold them over twice and then fold in the width sides to form a sealed packet with room for the steam.
6. Put the packets on the grill and grill for 10 to 12 minutes until the vegetables are tender-crisp and the fish flakes when tested with a fork. Be careful opening the packets because the escaping steam can be scalding.

NUTRITION: Per Serving: Calories: 267; Total fat: 12g; Saturated fat: 2g; Sodium: 97mg; Potassium: 582mg; Phosphorus: 238mg; Carbohydrates: 13g; Fiber: 2g; Protein: 29g; Sugar: 3g

97. Scrambled Eggs with Crab

Preparation Time: 10 minutes
Cooking Time: 8 minutes
Servings: 4
Difficulty: easy
INGREDIENTS

- 6 large eggs
- 4 egg whites
- ⅛ teaspoon freshly ground black pepper
- 2 tablespoons unsalted butter
- 1 red bell pepper, chopped
- 3 scallions, white and green parts, chopped

- 1 (6-ounce) can crab meat, drained
- ¼ cup shredded Swiss cheese
- 1 tablespoon chopped fresh chives

DIRECTIONS

1. In a medium bowl, whisk together the eggs, egg whites, and pepper until well blended and set aside.
2. Melt the butter in a large skillet over medium heat.
3. Sauté the red bell pepper and scallions for 2 minutes. Stir in the crab and cook for 1 minute longer. Remove this mixture from the skillet to a plate and set aside.
4. Add the beaten eggs to the skillet and cook, stirring occasionally, until the eggs form large curds and are set, about 2 to 4 minutes.
5. Add the vegetables and crab back to the eggs. Sprinkle with the cheese and cover the skillet for 1 minute to melt the cheese.
6. Remove the cover, sprinkle with the chives, and serve.

NUTRITION PER SERVING: Calories: 258; Total fat: 16g; Saturated fat: 7g; Sodium: 404mg; Potassium: 346mg; Phosphorus: 285mg; Carbohydrates: 4g; Fiber: 1g; Protein: 23g; Sugar: 3g

98. Grilled Cod

Preparation Time: 10 minutes
Cooking Time: 10 minutes
Servings: 4
Difficulty: easy
INGREDIENTS

- 2 (8 ounce) fillets cod, cut in half
- 1 tablespoon oregano
- ½ teaspoon lemon pepper
- ¼ teaspoon ground black pepper
- 2 tablespoons olive oil
- 1 lemon, juiced
- 2 tablespoons chopped green onion (white part only)

DIRECTIONS

1. Season both sides of cod with oregano, lemon pepper, and black pepper. Set fish aside on a plate. Heat butter in a small saucepan over medium heat, stir in lemon juice and green onion, and cook until onion is softened, about 3 minutes.
2. Place cod onto oiled grates and grill until fish is browned and flakes easily, about 3 minutes per side; baste with olive oil mixture frequently while grilling. Allow cod to rest of the heat for about 5 minutes before serving.

NUTRITION: Calories 92, Total Fat 7.4g, Saturated Fat 1g, Cholesterol 14mg, Sodium 19mg, Total Carbohydrate 2.5g, Dietary Fiber 1g, Total Sugars 0.5g, Protein 5.4g, Calcium 25mg, Iron 1mg, Potassium 50mg, Phosphorus 36 mg

99. Cod and Green Bean Curry

Preparation Time: 15 minutes
Cooking Time: 60 minutes
Servings: 4
Difficulty: easy

INGREDIENTS

- 1/2-pound green beans, trimmed and cut into bite-sized pieces
- 1 white onion, sliced
- 2 cloves garlic, minced
- 1 tablespoon olive oil, or more as needed
- Ground black pepper to taste
- Curry Mixture:
- 2 tablespoons water, or more as needed
- 2 teaspoons curry powder
- 2 teaspoons ground ginger
- 1 1/2 (6 ounce) cod fillets

DIRECTIONS

1. Preheat the oven to 400 degrees F.
2. Combine green beans, onion, and garlic in a large glass baking dish. Toss with olive oil to coat; season with the pepper.
3. Bake in the preheated oven, stirring occasionally, until edges of onion are slightly charred and green beans start to look dry, about 40 minutes. In the meantime, mix water, curry powder, and ginger together.
4. Remove dish and stir the vegetables; stir in curry mixture. Increase oven temperature to 450 degrees F.
5. Lay cod over the bottom of the dish and coat with vegetables. Continue baking until fish is opaque, 25 to 30 minutes depending on thickness.

NUTRITION: Calories 64, Total Fat 3.8g, Saturated Fat 0.5g, Cholesterol 0mg, Sodium 5mg, Total Carbohydrate 7.7g, Dietary Fiber 2.9g, Total Sugars 2g, Protein 1.6g, Calcium 35mg, Iron 1mg, Potassium 180mg, Phosphorus 101 mg

100. White Fish Soup

Preparation Time: 15 minutes
Cooking Time: 20 minutes
Servings: 4
Difficulty: easy
INGREDIENTS

- 2 tablespoons olive oil
- 1 onion, finely diced
- 1 green bell pepper, chopped
- 1 rib celery, thinly sliced
- 3 cups chicken broth, or more to taste
- 1/4 cup chopped fresh parsley
- 1 1/2 pounds cod, cut into 3/4-inch cubes
- Pepper to taste
- 1 dash red pepper flakes

DIRECTIONS

1. Heat oil in a soup pot over medium heat.
2. Add onion, bell pepper, and celery and cook until wilted, about 5 minutes.
3. Add broth and bring to a simmer, about 5 minutes.
4. Cook 15 to 20 minutes.
5. Add cod, parsley, and red pepper flakes and simmer until fish flakes easily with a fork, 8 to 10 minutes more.
6. Season with black pepper.

NUTRITION: Calories 117, Total Fat 7.2g, Saturated Fat 1.4g, Cholesterol 18mg, Sodium 37mg, Total Carbohydrate 5.4g, Dietary Fiber 1.3g, Total Sugars 2.8g, Protein 8.1g, Calcium 23mg, Iron 1mg, Potassium 122mg, Phosphorus 111 mg

101. Lemon- Rosemary Cod Fillets

Preparation time: 20 min
Cooking Time: 15 minutes
Servings: 4
Difficulty: easy
INGREDIENTS

- 4 egg whites, lightly beaten
- 2 lemons, sliced 1/4-inch thick
- 2 1/2 pounds skinless cod fillets
- 1 tablespoon olive oil
- 1/4 teaspoon black pepper
- 2 bunches fresh rosemary

DIRECTIONS

1. Preheat oven to 400 degrees F.
2. Add egg whites. Mix well with your hands or by blending with two spoons until the texture resembles moist sand.
3. Layer half of the prepared egg on the bottom of a glass 9x13-inch baking dish; pat down firmly. Place the lemon slices edge to edge on top of the egg. You don't want the fish to actually touch the salt or it will absorb too much; the lemon slices will serve as a barrier and a flavor infuser. Save extra lemon slices for serving and garnish.
4. Rub the fish fillets with olive oil on both sides, and pepper.
5. Arrange the fish fillets on top of the lemon slices, making sure no edges touch the salt base.
6. Arrange the rosemary on top so that it covers the fish completely, reserving a few sprigs to chop for garnish. Again, this will serve as a barrier against the crust since there is no skin to protect it from absorbing too much during baking, as well as give it a bold, tangy flavor.
7. Pour the rest of the mixture evenly onto the rosemary, smoothing carefully. Make sure all corners are covered; pat firmly to ensure a proper seal with no cracks.
8. Place in middle rack of oven and bake for 15 minutes.
9. Let fish rest for 5 minutes, then crack sides of salt crust with a strong knife before prying open.
10. Cut each fillet in half. Serve with remaining lemon slices and fresh, chopped rosemary.

NUTRITION: Calories 80, Total Fat 3.9g, Saturated Fat 0.6g, Cholesterol 12mg, Sodium 51mg, Total Carbohydrate 3.4g, Dietary Fiber 1.1g, Total Sugars 1g, Protein 8.8g, Calcium 21mg, Iron 1mg, Potassium 153mg, Phosphorus 110 mg

102. Onion Dijon Crusted Catfish

Preparation time: 5 min

Cooking Time: 25 minutes
Servings: 4
Difficulty: easy
INGREDIENTS

- 1 onion, finely chopped
- 1/4 cup honey Dijon mustard
- 4 (6 ounce) fillets catfish fillets
- Pepper to taste
- Dried parsley flakes

DIRECTIONS

1. Preheat the oven to 350 degrees F.
2. In a small bowl, mix together the onion and mustard. Season the catfish fillets with pepper. Place on a baking tray and coat with the onion and honey. Sprinkle parsley flakes over the top.
3. Bake for 20 minutes in the preheated oven, then turn the oven to broil. Broil until golden, 3 to 5 minutes.

NUTRITION: Calories 215, Total Fat 6.1g, Saturated Fat 1.7g, Cholesterol 87mg, Sodium 86mg, Total Carbohydrate 10.4g, Dietary Fiber 0.6g, Total Sugars 4.2g, Protein 31.6g, Calcium 8mg, Iron 0mg, Potassium 46mg, Phosphorus 30 mg

103. Herb Baked Tuna

Preparation time: 10 min
Cooking Time: 20 minutes
Servings: 4
Difficulty: easy
INGREDIENTS

- 4 (6 ounce) tuna fillets
- 2 tablespoons dried parsley
- 3/4 teaspoon paprika
- 1/2 teaspoon dried thyme
- 1/2 teaspoon dried oregano
- 1/2 teaspoon dried basil
- 1/2 teaspoon ground black pepper
- 2 tablespoons lemon juice
- 1 tablespoon olive oil
- 1/4 teaspoon garlic powder

DIRECTIONS

1. Preheat oven to 350 degrees F.
2. Arrange tuna fillets in a 9x13-inch baking dish. Combine parsley, paprika, thyme, oregano, basil, and black pepper in a small bowl; sprinkle herb mixture over fish. Mix lemon juice, olive oil, and garlic powder in another bowl; drizzle olive oil mixture over fish.
3. Bake in preheated oven until fish is easily flaked with a fork, about 20 minutes.

NUTRITION:
Calories 139, Total Fat 12.5g, Saturated Fat 0.6g, Cholesterol 0mg, Sodium 3mg, Total Carbohydrate 1g, Dietary Fiber 0.5g, Total Sugars 0.3g, Protein 6.2g, Calcium 11mg, Iron 1mg, Potassium 39mg, Phosphorus 20 mg

104. Cilantro Lime Salmon

Preparation time: 10 min
Cooking Time: 20 minutes
Servings: 4
Difficulty: easy
INGREDIENTS

- ¼ cup olive oil
- ¼ cup chopped fresh cilantro

- ½ teaspoon chopped garlic
- 5 (5 ounce) fillets salmon
- Ground black pepper to taste
- ½ lemon, juiced
- ½ lime, juiced

DIRECTIONS

1. Heat the olive oil in a skillet over medium heat.
2. Stir cilantro and garlic into the oil; cook about 1 minute.
3. Season salmon fillets with black pepper; lay gently into the oil mixture.
4. Place a cover on the skillet. Cook fillets 10 minutes, turn, and continue cooking until the fish flakes easily with a fork and is lightly browned, about 10 minutes more.
5. Squeeze lemon juice and lime juice over the fillets to serve.

NUTRITION: Calories 249, Total Fat 18.7g, Saturated Fat 3.3g, Cholesterol 18mg, Sodium 48mg, Total Carbohydrate 1.7g, Dietary Fiber 0.5g, Total Sugars 0.3g, Protein 20.7g, Calcium 6mg, Iron 0mg, Potassium 26mg, Phosphorus 20 mg

105. Asian Ginger tuna

Preparation time: 10 min
Cooking Time: 20 minutes
Servings: 4
Difficulty: easy

INGREDIENTS

- 1 cup water
- 1 tablespoon minced fresh ginger root
- 1 tablespoon minced garlic
- 2 tablespoons soy sauce
- 1 1/4 pounds thin tuna fillets
- 6 large white mushrooms, sliced
- 1/4 cup sliced green onion
- 1 tablespoon chopped fresh cilantro (optional)

DIRECTIONS

1. Put water, ginger, and garlic in a wide pot with a lid.
2. Bring the water to a boil, reduce heat to medium-low, and simmer 3 to 5 minutes.
3. Stir soy sauce into the water mixture; add tuna fillets.
4. Place cover on the pot, bring water to a boil, and let cook for 3 minutes more.
5. Add mushrooms, cover, and cook until the fish loses pinkness and begins to flake, about 3 minutes more.
6. Sprinkle green onion over the fillets, cover, and cook for 30 seconds.
7. Garnish with cilantro to serve.

NUTRITION: Calories 109, Total Fat 7.9g, Saturated Fat 0g, Cholesterol 0mg, Sodium 454mg, Total Carbohydrate 3.1g, Dietary Fiber 0.6g, Total Sugars 0.9g, Protein 7.1g, Calcium 10mg, Iron 1mg, Potassium 158mg, Phosphorus 120 mg

106. Cheesy Tuna Chowder

Preparation time: 10 min
Cooking Time: 20 minutes
Servings: 4

Difficulty: easy
INGREDIENTS

- 2 tablespoons olive oil
- 1/2 small onion, chopped
- 1 cup water
- 1/2 cup chopped celery
- 1 cup sliced baby carrots
- 3 cups soy milk, divided
- 1/3 cup all-purpose flour
- 1/2 teaspoon ground black pepper
- 1 1/2 pounds tuna fillets, cut into 1-inch pieces
- 1 1/2 cups shredded Cheddar cheese

DIRECTIONS

1. In a Dutch oven over medium heat, heat olive oil and sauté the onion until tender. Pour in water. Mix in celery, carrots, and cook 10 minutes, stirring occasionally, until vegetables are tender.
2. In a small bowl, whisk together 1 1/2 cups milk and all-purpose flour. Mix into the Dutch oven.
3. Mix remaining milk, and pepper into the Dutch oven. Stirring occasionally, continue cooking the mixture about 10 minutes, until thickened.
4. Stir tuna into the mixture, and cook 5 minutes, or until fish is easily flaked with a fork. Mix in Cheddar cheese, and cook another 5 minutes, until melted.

NUTRITION: Calories 228, Total Fat 15.5g, Saturated Fat 6.5g, Cholesterol 30mg, Sodium 206mg, Total Carbohydrate 10.8g, Dietary Fiber 1g, Total Sugars 4.1g, Protein 11.6g, Calcium 183mg, Iron 1mg, Potassium 163mg, Phosphorus 150 mg

107. Lemon Butter Salmon

Preparation Time: 15 minutes
Cooking Time: 15 minutes
Servings: 6
Difficulty: easy
INGREDIENTS

- 1 tablespoon butter
- 2 tablespoons olive oil
- 1 tablespoon Dijon mustard
- 1 tablespoons lemon juice
- 2 cloves garlic, crushed
- 1 teaspoon dried dill
- 1 teaspoon dried basil leaves
- 1 tablespoon capers
- 24-ounce salmon filet

DIRECTIONS

1. Put all the ingredients except the salmon in a saucepan over medium heat.
2. Bring to a boil and then simmer for 5 minutes.
3. Preheat your grill.
4. Create a packet using foil.
5. Place the sauce and salmon inside.
6. Seal the packet.
7. Grill for 12 minutes.

NUTRITION: Calories 294 Protein 23 g Carbohydrates 1 g Fat 22 g Cholesterol 68 mg Sodium 190 mg Potassium 439 mg Phosphorus 280 mg Calcium 21 mg

108. Tofu Stir Fry

Preparation Time: 15 minutes
Cooking Time: 20 minutes
Servings: 4
Difficulty: easy

INGREDIENTS

- 1 teaspoon sugar
- 1 tablespoon lime juice
- 1 tablespoon low sodium soy sauce
- 2 tablespoons cornstarch
- 2 egg whites, beaten
- 1/2 cup unseasoned bread crumbs
- 1 tablespoon vegetable oil
- 16 ounces tofu, cubed
- 1 clove garlic, minced
- 1 tablespoon sesame oil
- 1 red bell pepper, sliced into strips
- 1 cup broccoli florets
- 1 teaspoon herb seasoning blend
- Dash black pepper
- Sesame seeds
- Steamed white rice

DIRECTIONS

1. Dissolve sugar in a mixture of lime juice and soy sauce. Set aside.
2. In the first bowl, put the cornstarch.
3. Add the egg whites in the second bowl.
4. Place the breadcrumbs in the third bowl.
5. Dip each tofu cubes in the first, second and third bowls.
6. Pour vegetable oil in a pan over medium heat.
7. Cook tofu cubes until golden.
8. Drain the tofu and set aside.
9. Remove oil from the pan and add sesame oil.
10. Add garlic, bell pepper and broccoli.
11. Cook until crisp tender.
12. Season with the seasoning blend and pepper.
13. Put the tofu back and toss to mix.
14. Pour soy sauce mixture on top and transfer to serving bowls.
15. Garnish with the sesame seeds and serve on top of white rice.

NUTRITION: Calories 400 Protein 19 g Carbohydrates 45 g Fat 16 g Cholesterol 0 mg Sodium 584 mg Potassium 317 mg Phosphorus 177 mg Calcium 253 mg Fiber 2.7 g

109. Broccoli Pancake

Preparation Time: 10 minutes
Cooking Time: 5 minutes
Servings: 4
Difficulty: easy

INGREDIENTS

- 3 cups broccoli florets, diced
- 2 eggs, beaten
- 2 tablespoons all-purpose flour
- 1/2 cup onion, chopped
- 2 tablespoons olive oil

DIRECTIONS

1. Boil broccoli in water for 5 minutes. Drain and set aside.
2. Mix egg and flour.
3. Add onion and broccoli to the mixture.
4. Pour oil in a pan over medium heat.
5. Cook the broccoli pancake until brown on both sides.

NUTRITION: Calories 140 Protein 6 g Carbohydrates 7 g Fat 10 g Cholesterol 106 mg Sodium 58 mg Potassium 276 mg Phosphorus 101 mg Calcium 50 mg Fiber 2.1 g

110. Carrot Casserole

Preparation Time: 10 minutes
Cooking Time: 20 minutes
Serving: 8
Difficulty: easy
INGREDIENTS

- 1-pound carrots, sliced into rounds
- 12 low-sodium crackers
- 2 tablespoons butter
- 2 tablespoons onion, chopped
- 1/4 cup cheddar cheese, shredded

DIRECTIONS

1. Preheat your oven to 350 degrees F.
2. Boil carrots in a pot of water until tender.
3. Drain the carrots and reserve ¼ cup liquid.
4. Mash carrots.
5. Add all the ingredients into the carrots except cheese.
6. Place the mashed carrots in a casserole dish.
7. Sprinkle cheese on top and bake in the oven for 15 minutes.

NUTRITION: Calories 94 Protein 2 g Carbohydrates 9 g Fat 6 g Cholesterol 13 mg Sodium 174 mg Potassium 153 mg Phosphorus 47 mg Calcium 66 mg Fiber 1.8 g

111. Cauliflower Rice

Preparation Time: 10 minutes
Cooking Time: 10 minutes
Servings: 4
Difficulty: easy
INGREDIENTS

- 1 head cauliflower, sliced into florets
- 1 tablespoon butter
- Black pepper to taste
- 1/4 teaspoon garlic powder
- 1/4 teaspoon herb seasoning blend

DIRECTIONS

1. Put cauliflower florets in a food processor.

2. Pulse until consistency is similar to grain.
3. In a pan over medium heat, melt the butter and add the spices.
4. Toss cauliflower rice and cook for 10 minutes.
5. Fluff using a fork before serving.

NUTRITION: Calories 47 Protein 1 g Carbohydrates 4 g Fat 3 g Cholesterol 8 mg Sodium 43 mg Potassium 206 mg Phosphorus 31 mg Calcium 16 mg Fiber 1.4 g

112. Eggplant Fries

Preparation Time: 10 minutes
Cooking Time: 5 minutes
Servings: 6
Difficulty: easy
INGREDIENTS
- 2 eggs, beaten
- 1 cup almond milk
- 1 teaspoon hot sauce
- 3/4 cup cornstarch
- 3 teaspoons dry ranch seasoning mix
- 3/4 cup dry bread crumbs
- 1 eggplant, sliced into strips
- 1/2 cup oil

DIRECTIONS
1. In a bowl, mix eggs, milk and hot sauce.
2. In a dish, mix cornstarch, seasoning and breadcrumbs.
3. Dip first the eggplant strips in the egg mixture.
4. Coat each strip with the cornstarch mixture.

5. Pour oil in a pan over medium heat.
6. Once hot, add the fries and cook for 3 minutes or until golden.

NUTRITION: Calories 233 Protein 5 g Carbohydrates 24 g Fat 13 g Cholesterol 48 mg Sodium 212 mg Potassium 215 mg Phosphorus 86 mg Calcium 70 mg Fiber 2.1 g

113. Seasoned Green Beans

Preparation Time: 10 minutes
Cooking Time: 10 minutes
Servings: 4
Difficulty: easy
INGREDIENTS
- 10-ounce green beans
- 4 teaspoons butter
- 1/4 cup onion, chopped
- 1/2 cup red bell pepper, chopped
- 1 teaspoon dried dill weed
- 1 teaspoon dried parsley
- 1/4 teaspoon black pepper

DIRECTIONS
1. Boil green beans in a pot of water. Drain.
2. In a pan over medium heat, melt the butter and cook onion and bell pepper.
3. Season with dill and parsley.
4. Put the green beans back to the skillet.
5. Sprinkle pepper on top before serving.

NUTRITION: Calories 67 Protein 2 g Carbohydrates 8 g Fat 3 g Cholesterol 0 mg Sodium 55 mg Potassium 194 mg

Phosphorus 32 mg Calcium 68 mg Fiber 4.0 g

114. Grilled Squash

Preparation Time: 10 minutes
Cooking Time: 6 minutes
Servings: 8
Difficulty: easy
INGREDIENTS

- 4 zucchinis, rinsed, drained and sliced
- 4 crookneck squash, rinsed, drained and sliced
- Cooking spray
- 1/4 teaspoon garlic powder
- 1/4 teaspoon black pepper

DIRECTIONS

1. Arrange squash on a baking sheet.
2. Spray with oil.
3. Season with garlic powder and pepper.
4. Grill for 3 minutes per side or until tender but not too soft.

NUTRITION: Calories 17 Protein 1 g Carbohydrates 3 g Fat 0 g Cholesterol 0 mg Sodium 6 mg Potassium 262 mg Phosphorus 39 mg Calcium 16 mg Fiber 1.1 g

115. Thai Tofu Broth

Preparation time: 5 minutes
Cooking time: 15 minutes
Servings: 4
Difficulty: easy
INGREDIENTS

- 1 cup rice noodles
- ½ sliced onion
- 6 ounce drained, pressed and cubed tofu
- ¼ cup sliced scallions
- ½ cup water
- ½ cup canned water chestnuts
- ½ cup rice milk
- 1 tablespoon lime juice
- 1 tablespoon coconut oil
- ½ finely sliced chili
- 1 cup snow peas

DIRECTIONS

1. Heat the oil in a wok on a high heat and then sauté the tofu until brown on each side.
2. Add the onion and sauté for 2-3 minutes.
3. Add the rice milk and water to the wok until bubbling.
4. Lower to medium heat and add the noodles, chili and water chestnuts.
5. Allow to simmer for 10-15 minutes and then add the sugar snap peas for 5 minutes.
6. Serve with a sprinkle of scallions.

NUTRITION: Calories 304, Protein 9 g, Carbs 38 g, Fat 13 g, Sodium (Na) 36 mg, Potassium (K) 114 mg, Phosphorus 101 mg

116. Delicious Vegetarian Lasagna

Preparation time: 10 minutes
Cooking time: 1 hour
Servings: 4
Difficulty: easy

INGREDIENTS

- 1 teaspoon basil
- 1 tablespoon olive oil
- ½ sliced red pepper
- 3 lasagna sheets
- ½ diced red onion
- ¼ teaspoon black pepper
- 1 cup rice milk
- 1 minced garlic clove
- 1 cup sliced eggplant
- ½ sliced zucchini
- ½ pack soft tofu
- 1 teaspoon oregano

DIRECTIONS

1. Preheat oven to 325°F/Gas Mark 3.
2. Slice zucchini, eggplant and pepper into vertical strips.
3. Add the rice milk and tofu to a food processor and blitz until smooth. Set aside.
4. Heat the oil in a skillet over medium heat and add the onions and garlic for 3-4 minutes or until soft.
5. Sprinkle in the herbs and pepper and allow to stir through for 5-6 minutes until hot.
6. Into a lasagna or suitable oven dish, layer 1 lasagna sheet, then 1/3 the eggplant, followed by 1/3 zucchini, then 1/3 pepper before pouring over 1/3 of tofu white sauce.
7. Repeat for the next 2 layers, finishing with the white sauce.
8. Add to the oven for 40-50 minutes or until veg is soft and can easily be sliced into servings.

NUTRITION: Calories 235, Protein 5 g, Carbs 10g, Fat 9 g, Sodium (Na) 35 mg, Potassium (K) 129 mg, Phosphorus 66 mg

117. Chili Tofu Noodles

Preparation time: 5 minutes
Cooking Time: 15 minutes
Servings: 4
Difficulty: easy

INGREDIENTS

- ½ diced red chili
- 2 cups rice noodles
- ½ juiced lime
- 6 ounce pressed and cubed silken firm tofu
- 1 teaspoon grated fresh ginger
- 1 tablespoon coconut oil
- 1 cup green beans
- 1 minced garlic clove

DIRECTIONS

1. Steam the green beans for 10-12 minutes or according to package **directions** and drain.
2. Cook the noodles in a pot of boiling water for 10-15 minutes or according to package **directions**.
3. Meanwhile, heat a wok or skillet on a high heat and add coconut oil.
4. Now add the tofu, chili flakes, garlic and ginger and sauté for 5-10 minutes.
5. Drain the noodles and add to the wok along with the green beans and lime juice.
6. Toss to coat.
7. Serve hot!

NUTRITION: Calories 246, Protein 10 g, Carbs 28g, Fat 12 g, Sodium (Na) 25 mg, Potassium (K) 126 mg, Phosphorus 79 mg

118. Curried Cauliflower

Preparation time: 5 minutes
Cooking time: 20 minutes
Servings: 4
Difficulty: easy
INGREDIENTS

- 1 teaspoon turmeric
- 1 diced onion
- 1 tablespoon chopped fresh cilantro
- 1 teaspoon cumin
- ½ diced chili
- ½ cup water
- 1 minced garlic clove
- 1 tablespoon coconut oil
- 1 teaspoon garam masala
- 2 cups cauliflower florets

DIRECTIONS

1. Add the oil to a skillet on medium heat.
2. Sauté the onion and garlic for 5 minutes until soft.
3. Add the cumin, turmeric and garam masala and stir to release the aromas.
4. Now add the chili to the pan along with the cauliflower.
5. Stir to coat.
6. Pour in the water and reduce the heat to a simmer for 15 minutes.
7. Garnish with cilantro to serve.

NUTRITION: Calories 108, Protein 2 g, Carbs 11 g, Fat 7 g, Sodium (Na) 35 mg, Potassium (K) 328 mg, Phosphorus 39 mg

119. Elegant Veggie Tortillas

Preparation Time: 30 minutes
Cooking Time: 15 minutes
Servings: 12
Difficulty: easy
INGREDIENTS

- 1½ cups of chopped broccoli florets
- 1½ cups of chopped cauliflower florets
- 1 tablespoon of water
- 2 teaspoon of canola oil
- 1½ cups of chopped onion
- 1 minced garlic clove
- 2 tablespoons of finely chopped fresh parsley
- 1 cup of low-cholesterol liquid egg substitute
- Freshly ground black pepper, to taste
- 4 (6-ounce) warmed corn tortillas

DIRECTIONS

1. In a microwave bowl, place broccoli, cauliflower and water and microwave, covered for about 3-5 minutes.
2. Remove from microwave and drain any liquid.
3. In a skillet, heat oil on medium heat.
4. Add onion and sauté for about 4-5 minutes.
5. Add garlic and sauté for about 1 minute.

6. Stir in broccoli, cauliflower, parsley, egg substitute and black pepper.
7. Reduce the heat to medium-low and simmer for about 10 minutes.
8. Remove from heat and keep aside to cool slightly.
9. Place broccoli mixture over ¼ of each tortilla.
10. Fold the outside edges inward and roll up like a burrito.
11. Secure each tortilla with toothpicks to secure the filling.
12. Cut each tortilla in half and serve.

NUTRITION: Per Serving, Calories: 217-Fat: 3.3g - Carbs: 41g - Protein: 8.1g - Fiber: 6.3g - Potassium: 289mg - Sodium: 87mg

120. Simple Broccoli Stir-Fry

Preparation Time: 40 minutes
Cooking Time: 15 minutes
Servings: 4
Difficulty: easy
Difficulty: easy
INGREDIENTS
- 1 tablespoon of olive oil
- 1 minced garlic clove
- 2 cups of broccoli florets
- 2 tablespoons of water

DIRECTIONS
1. In a large skillet, heat oil on medium heat.
2. Add garlic and sauté for about 1 minute.
3. Add broccoli and stir fry for about 2 minutes.

4. Stir in water and stir fry for about 4-5 minutes.
5. Serve warm.

NUTRITION: Per Serving, Calories: 47-Fat: 3.6g - Carbs: 3.3g - Protein: 1.3g - Fiber: 1.2g - Potassium: 147mg - Sodium: 15mg

121. Braised Cabbage

Preparation Time: 30 minutes
Cooking Time: 15 minutes
Servings: 4
Difficulty: easy
INGREDIENTS
- 1½ teaspoon of olive oil
- 2 minced garlic cloves
- 1 thinly sliced onion
- 3 cups of chopped green cabbage
- 1 cup of low-sodium vegetable broth
- Freshly ground black pepper, to taste

DIRECTIONS
1. In a large skillet, heat oil on medium-high heat.
2. Add garlic and sauté for about 1 minute.
3. Add onion and sauté for about 4-5 minutes.
4. Add cabbage and sauté for about 3-4 minutes.
5. Stir in broth and black pepper and immediately, reduce the heat to low.
6. Cook, covered for about 20 minutes.
7. Serve warm.

NUTRITION: Per Serving, Calories: 45-Fat: 1.8g - Carbs: 6.6g - Protein: 1.1g - Fiber: 1.9g - Potassium: 136mg - Sodium: 46mg

122. Salad with Strawberries and Goat Cheese

Preparation Time: 15 Minutes
Cooking time: 0 minute
Servings: 2
Difficulty: easy
INGREDIENTS

- Baby lettuce, to taste
- 1-pint strawberries
- Balsamic vinegar
- Extra virgin olive oil
- 1/4 teaspoon black pepper
- 8-ounce soft goat cheese

DIRECTIONS

1. Prepare the lettuce by washing and drying it, then cut the strawberries.
2. Cut the soft goat cheese into 8 pieces.
3. Put together the balsamic vinegar and the extra virgin olive oil in a large cup with a whisk.
4. Mix the strawberries pressing them and putting them in a bowl, add the dressing and mix, then divide the lettuce into four dishes and cut the other strawberries, arranging them on the salad.
5. Put cheese slices on top and add pepper. Serve and enjoy!

NUTRITION: Calories: 300 Protein: 13 g Sodium: 285 mg Potassium: 400 mg Phosphorus: 193 mg

123. Roasted Veggies Mediterranean Style

Preparation Time: 5 minutes
Cooking Time: 10 minutes
Servings: 2
Difficulty: easy
INGREDIENTS

- ½ teaspoon freshly grated lemon zest
- 1 cup grape tomatoes
- 1 tablespoon extra-virgin olive oil
- 1 tablespoon lemon juice
- 1 teaspoon dried oregano
- 10 pitted black olives, sliced
- 12-ounce broccoli crowns, trimmed and cut into bite-sized pieces
- 2 cloves garlic, minced
- 2 teaspoons capers, rinsed

DIRECTIONS

1. Preheat oven to 350oF and grease a baking sheet with cooking spray.
2. In a large bowl toss together until thoroughly coated salt, garlic, oil, tomatoes and broccoli. Spread broccoli on prepped baking sheet and bake for 8 to 10 minutes.
3. In another large bowl mix capers, oregano, olives, lemon juice, and lemon zest. Mix in roasted vegetables and serve while still warm.

NUTRITION: Calories: 110; carbs: 16g; protein: 6g; fats: 4g; phosphorus: 138mg; potassium: 745mg; sodium: 214mg

124. Fruity Garden Lettuce Salad

Preparation Time: 10 minutes
Cooking Time: 0 minutes
Servings: 4
Difficulty: easy

INGREDIENTS

- ¼ cup apple cider vinegar
- ¼ cup chopped almonds
- ½ avocado, thinly sliced
- ½ cup extra virgin olive oil
- ½ lemon, juiced
- 1 teaspoon ground black pepper
- 2 Granny Smith apples, thinly sliced
- 2 teaspoons grainy mustard
- 6 cups thinly sliced lettuce

DIRECTIONS

1. In a large salad bowl, toss lemon juice and apples. Mix in almonds, avocado, and lettuce.
2. In a small bowl mix salt, pepper, mustard, vinegar and olive oil until salt is thoroughly dissolved.
3. Pour dressing over lettuce mixture and toss well to combine. Serve and enjoy.

NUTRITION: Calories: 123; carbs: 16.5g; protein: 2g; fats: 6g; phosphorus: 56mg; potassium: 450mg; sodium: 35mg

125. Baked Dilly Pickerel

Preparation Time: 5 Mins
Cooking Time: 15 Mins
Servings: 3
Difficulty: easy

INGREDIENTS

- 4 Fillets of pickerel, about 4 ounces
- For the dilly Sauce
- ½ package of whipped cream cheese
- 4 Minced garlic cloves
- ½ Diced small onion
- 3 tablespoons of fresh or dried dill
- ½ teaspoon of ground pepper

DIRECTIONS

1. Preheat your oven to a temperature of 350°F.
2. Mix the ingredients of the dilly sauce very well to make a paste.
3. Line a baking pan with a tin foil; then set the fish and spread the dilly sauce on its top
4. Cover the fish with an aluminum foil tin and bake it for about 15 minutes in the oven
5. Serve and enjoy your dinner!

NUTRITION: Calories: 295.6, Fats: 18.7g, Carbs: 11g, Fiber: 2.2g, Potassium: 140mg, Sodium: 6.8mg, Phosphorous: 58g, Protein 20.7g

126. Rice Salad

Preparation Time: 10 minutes
Cooking Time: 20 minutes
Servings: 2
Difficulty: easy

INGREDIENTS

- 1 Cup of olive oil
- ½ Cup of balsamic vinegar
- 1 teaspoon of lemon juice
- ¾ teaspoons of black pepper
- 3 Minced garlic cloves

- ½ teaspoon of dried basil
- ½ teaspoon of dried oregano
- ½ Cup of fresh parsley
- 2 cups of bell peppers
- ½ Cup of chopped red onion
- 1 Cup of frozen artichoke hearts
- 1/3 Cup of fresh dill weed
- 6 Cups of cooked white rice
- 1 Pound of cooked shrimp
- ½ Cup of dried cranberries
- 8 Ounces of canned pineapple chunks
- 1 Cup of frozen green peas

DIRECTIONS

1. To make the dressing, whisk all together the oil with the vinegar, the salt, the pepper, the minced garlic, the basil, the oregano and about ¼ cup of chopped parsley; then set the mixture aside.
2. Chop the red bell peppers and the onion; then mince the dill weed
3. Cook your ingredients and quarter the artichoke hearts.
4. In a large bowl combine the rice with the shrimp, the bell peppers, the onion, the artichoke hearts, and ½ cup of minced parsley, the dill, the cranberries, the pineapple and the green peas.
5. Stir the dressing into the salad and let it chill for about 2 hours to marinate.
6. Serve and enjoy your dinner over a bed of lettuce!

NUTRITION: Calories: 165.4, Fats: 11g, Carbs: 8g, Fiber: 0.89g, Potassium: 181mg, Sodium: 99mg, Phosphorous: 75g, Protein 8g

127. Baked Eggplant Tray

Preparation time: 10 minutes
Cooking Time: 20 minutes
Servings: 2
Difficulty: Medium
INGREDIENTS
3 Cups of eggplant
- 3 large omega-3 eggs
- ½ Cup of liquid non-dairy creamer
- 1 teaspoon of vinegar
- 1 Teaspoon of lemon juice
- ½ teaspoon of pepper
- ¼ teaspoon of sage
- ½ Cup of white breadcrumbs
- 1 tablespoon of margarine

DIRECTIONS

1. Preheat your oven to a temperature of about 350° F
2. Peel the eggplant and cut it into pieces
3. Place the eggplant pieces in a large pan; then cover it with water and let boil until it becomes tender
4. Drain the eggplants and mash it very well
5. Combine the beaten eggs with the non-dairy creamer, the vinegar, the lemon juice, the pepper and the sage with the mashed eggplant; then place it into a greased baking tray

6. Mix the melted margarine with the breadcrumbs.
7. Top you tray with the breadcrumbs and bake it for about 20 minutes
8. Set the tray aside to cool for about 5 minutes
9. Serve and enjoy your dinner!

NUTRITION: Calories: 126, Fats: 8g, Carbs: 4.7g, Fiber: 1.6g, Potassium: 224mg, Sodium: 143mg, Phosphorous: 115g, Protein 7.3g

128. Raw Vegetables. Chopped Salad

Preparation Time: 15 minutes
Cooking Time: 0 minute
Servings: 4
Difficulty: Medium
INGREDIENTS

- Chopped raw veggie salad
- 1 orange pepper (minced) (about 1 cup)
- 1 yellow pepper (small cut) (about 1 cup)
- 5-8 radishes (halve and cut into thin slices) (about 3/4 cup)
- small head of broccoli (minced) (about 2 cups)
- 1 seedless cucumber (small cut) (about 2 cups)
- 1 cup of halved red seedless grapes
- 2-3 tablespoons chopped fresh dill
- 1/4 cup chopped fresh parsley
- 1/4 cup of raw peeled sunflower seeds
- 1/8 cup raw hemp hearts (peeled hemp seeds)
- Oil-free dressing
- garlic clove (chopped)
- tablespoons of red wine vinegar
- 1 tablespoon of apple cider vinegar
- Juice of 1 lemon
- 1 tablespoon Dijonsenf
- 1 tablespoon pure maple syrup
- 1/2 teaspoon salt (or to taste)
- 1/8 teaspoon pepper (or to taste)

DIRECTIONS

1. Whisk the ingredients - Chopped raw veggie salad, 1 orange pepper, yellow pepper, radishes, small head of broccoli, seedless cucumber, halved red seedless grapes, chopped fresh dill, chopped fresh parsley, raw peeled sunflower seeds, raw hemp hearts, garlic clove, red wine vinegar, apple cider vinegar, lemon, Dijonsenf, pure maple syrup, salt, pepper. For dressing in a small bowl and set aside.
2. Combine all the salad **ingredients** in a large bowl.
3. Pour the dressing over the chopped vegetables and wrap well.
4. Cover and then refrigerate it for an hour or two and toss the salad once or twice during this time to coat evenly. Enjoy!

NUTRITION: Calories: 111 Total Fat: 2g Saturated Fat: 1g Cholesterol: 10mg Sodium: 58mg Carbohydrates: 19g Sugar: 18 g Calcium: 15%

129. Roasted Citrus Chicken

Preparation Time: 20mins
Cooking Time: 60mins
Servings: 8
Difficulty: Medium
INGREDIENTS

- 1 - Tablespoon olive oil
- 2 - cloves garlic, minced
- 1 - teaspoon Italian seasoning
- ½ - teaspoon black pepper
- 8 - chicken thighs
- 2 - cups chicken broth, reduced-sodium
- 3 - Tablespoons lemon juice
- ½ - large chicken breast for 1 chicken thigh

DIRECTIONS

1. Warm oil in huge skillet.
2. Include garlic and seasonings.
3. Include chicken bosoms and dark-colored all sides.
4. Spot chicken in the moderate cooker and include the chicken soup.
5. Cook on LOW heat for 6 to 8hours
6. Include lemon juice toward the part of the bargain time.

NUTRITION: Calories: 265 Fat: 19g Protein: 21g Carbs: 1g

130. Chicken with Asian Vegetables

Preparation Time: 10mins
Cooking Time: 20mins
Servings: 8
Difficulty: Medium
INGREDIENTS

- 2 - Tablespoons canola oil
- 6 - boneless chicken breasts
- 1 - cup low-sodium chicken broth
- 3 - Tablespoons reduced-sodium soy sauce
- ¼ - teaspoon crushed red pepper flakes
- 1 - garlic clove, crushed
- 1 - can (8ounces) water chestnuts, sliced and rinsed (optional)
- ½ - cup sliced green onions
- 1 - cup chopped red or green bell pepper
- 1 - cup chopped celery
- ¼ - cup cornstarch
- ⅓ - cup water
- 3 - cups cooked white rice
- ½ - large chicken breast for 1 chicken thigh

DIRECTIONS

1. Warm oil in a skillet and dark-colored chicken on all sides.

2. Add chicken to slow cooker with the remainder of the fixings aside from cornstarch and water.
3. Spread and cook on LOW for 6 to 8hours
4. Following 6-8 hours, independently blend cornstarch and cold water until smooth. Gradually include into the moderate cooker.
5. At that point turn on high for about 15mins until thickened. Don't close top on the moderate cooker to enable steam to leave.
6. Serve Asian blend over rice.

NUTRITION: Calories: 415 Fat: 20g Protein: 20g Carbs: 36g

131. Chicken Adobo

Preparation Time: 10mins
Cooking Time: 1hr 40mins
Servings: 6
Difficulty: Medium
INGREDIENTS
- 4 - medium yellow onions, halved and thinly sliced
- 4 - medium garlic cloves, smashed and peeled
- 1 - (5-inch) piece fresh ginger, cut into
- 1 - inch pieces
- 1 - bay leaf
- 3 - pounds bone-in chicken thighs
- 3 - Tablespoons reduced-sodium soy sauce
- ¼ - cup rice vinegar (not seasoned)
- 1 - Tablespoon granulated sugar
- ½ - teaspoon freshly ground black pepper

DIRECTIONS
1. Spot the onions, garlic, ginger, and narrows leaf in an even layer in the slight cooker.
2. Take out and do away with the pores and skin from the chicken.
3. Organize the hen in an even layer over the onion mixture.
4. Whisk the soy sauce, vinegar, sugar, and pepper collectively in a medium bowl and pour it over the fowl.
5. Spread and prepare dinner on LOW for 8hours
6. Evacuate and take away the ginger portions and inlet leaf.
7. Present with steamed rice.

NUTRITION: Calories318 Fat: 9g Protein: 14g Carbs: 44g

132. Chicken and Veggie Soup

Preparation Time: 15mins
Cooking Time: 25mins
Servings: 8
Difficulty: Medium
INGREDIENTS
- 4 - cups cooked and chopped chicken

- 7 - cups reduced-sodium chicken broth
- 1 - pound frozen white corn
- 1 - medium onion diced
- 4 - cloves garlic minced
- 2 - carrots peeled and diced
- 2 - celery stalks chopped
- 2 - teaspoons oregano
- 2 - teaspoon curry powder
- ½ - teaspoon black pepper

DIRECTIONS

1. Include all fixings into the moderate cooker.
2. Cook on LOW for 8hours
3. Serve over cooked white rice.

NUTRITION: Calories220 Fat: 7g Protein: 24g Carbs: 19g

133. Turkey Sausages

Preparation Time: 10 Minutes
Cooking time: 10 minutes
Servings: 2
Difficulty: Medium
INGREDIENTS

- 1/4 teaspoon salt
- 1/8 teaspoon garlic powder
- 1/8 teaspoon onion powder
- 1 teaspoon fennel seed
- 1 pound 7% fat ground turkey

DIRECTIONS

1. Press the fennel seed and in a small cup put together turkey with fennel seed, garlic and onion powder and salt.
2. Cover the bowl and refrigerate overnight.

3. Prepare the turkey with seasoning into different portions with a circle form and press them into patties ready to be cooked.
4. Cook at a medium heat until browned.
5. Cook it for 1 to 2 minutes per side and serve them hot. Enjoy!

NUTRITION: Calories: 55 Protein: 7 g Sodium: 70 mg Potassium: 105 mg Phosphorus: 75 mg

134. Rosemary Chicken

Preparation Time: 10 Minutes
Cooking time: 10 minutes
Servings: 2
Difficulty: Medium
INGREDIENTS

- 2 zucchinis
- 1 carrot
- 1 teaspoon dried rosemary
- 4 chicken breasts
- 1/2 bell pepper
- 1/2 red onion
- 8 garlic cloves
- Olive oil
- 1/4 tablespoon ground pepper

DIRECTIONS

1. Prepare the oven and preheat it at 375 °F (or 200°C).
2. Slice both zucchini and carrots and add bell pepper, onion, garlic and put everything adding oil in a 13" x 9" pan.
3. Spread the pepper over everything and roast for about 10 minutes.

4. Meanwhile, lift up the chicken skin and spread black pepper and rosemary on the flesh.
5. Remove the vegetable pan from the oven and add the chicken, returning the pan to the oven for about 30 more minutes. Serve and enjoy!

NUTRITION: Calories: 215 Protein: 28 g Sodium: 105 mg Potassium: 580 mg Phosphorus: 250 mg

135. Smoky Turkey Chili

Preparation Time: 5 minutes
Cooking Time: 45 minutes
Servings: 8
Difficulty: Medium
INGREDIENTS
- 12ounce lean ground turkey
- 1/2 red onion, chopped
- 2 cloves garlic, crushed and chopped
- ½ teaspoon of smoked paprika
- ½ teaspoon of chili powder
- ½ teaspoon of dried thyme
- ¼ cup reduced-sodium beef stock
- ½ cup of water
- 1 ½ cups baby spinach leaves, washed
- 3 wheat tortillas

DIRECTIONS
1. Brown the ground beef in a dry skillet over a medium-high heat.
2. Add in the red onion and garlic.
3. Sauté the onion until it goes clear.
4. Transfer the contents of the skillet to the slow cooker.

5. Add the remaining **ingredients** and simmer on Low for 30–45 minutes.
6. Stir through the spinach for the last few minutes to wilt.
7. Slice tortillas and gently toast under the broiler until slightly crispy.
8. Serve on top of the turkey chili.

NUTRITION: Per Serving: Calories: 93.5 Protein: 8g Carbohydrates: 3g Fat: 5.5g Cholesterol: 30.5mg Sodium: 84.5mg Potassium: 142.5mg Phosphorus: 92.5mgCalcium: 29mg Fiber: 0.5g

136. Avocado-Orange Grilled Chicken

Preparation Time: 20 minutes
Cooking Time: 60 minutes
Servings: 4
Difficulty: Medium
INGREDIENTS
- ¼ cup fresh lime juice
- ¼ cup minced red onion
- 1 avocado
- 1 cup low fat yogurt
- 1 small red onion, sliced thinly
- 1 tablespoon honey
- 2 oranges, peeled and sectioned
- 2 tablespoons. chopped cilantro
- 4 pieces of 4-6ounce boneless, skinless chicken breasts
- Pepper and salt to taste

DIRECTIONS
1. In a large bowl mix honey, cilantro, minced red onion and yogurt.
2. Submerge chicken into mixture and marinate for at least 30 minutes.

3. Grease grate and preheat grill to medium high fire.
4. Remove chicken from marinade and season with pepper and salt.
5. Grill for 6 minutes per side or until chicken is cooked and juices run clear.
6. Meanwhile, peel avocado and discard seed. Chop avocados and place in bowl. Quickly add lime juice and toss avocado to coat well with juice.
7. Add cilantro, thinly sliced onions and oranges into bowl of avocado, mix well.
8. Serve grilled chicken and avocado dressing on the side.

NUTRITION: Calories per Serving: 209; carbs: 26g; protein: 8g; fats: 10g; phosphorus: 157mg; potassium: 548mg; sodium: 125mg

137. Herbs and Lemony Roasted Chicken

Preparation Time: 15 minutes
Cooking Time: 1 ½ hours
Servings: 8
Difficulty: Medium
INGREDIENTS
- ½ teaspoon ground black pepper
- ½ teaspoon mustard powder
- ½ teaspoon salt
- 1 3-lb whole chicken
- 1 teaspoon garlic powder
- 2 lemons
- 2 tablespoons. olive oil

- 2 teaspoons. Italian seasoning

DIRECTIONS
1. In small bowl, mix well black pepper, garlic powder, mustard powder, and salt.
2. Rinse chicken well and slice off giblets.
3. In a greased 9 x 13 baking dish, place chicken and add 1 ½ teaspoons. of seasoning made earlier inside the chicken and rub the remaining seasoning around chicken.
4. In small bowl, mix olive oil and juice from 2 lemons. Drizzle over chicken.
5. Bake chicken in a preheated 350oF oven until juices run clear, around 1 ½ hours. Every once in a while, baste chicken with its juices.

NUTRITION: Calories per Serving: 190; carbs: 2g; protein: 35g; fats: 9g; phosphorus: 341mg; potassium: 439mg; sodium: 328mg

138. Ground Chicken & Peas Curry

Preparation Time: 15 minutes
Cooking Time: 6-10 minutes
Servings: 3-4
Difficulty: Medium
INGREDIENTS
For Marinade:
- 3 tablespoons essential olive oil
- 2 bay leaves
- 2 onions, grinded to some paste
- ½ tablespoon garlic paste
- ½ tablespoon ginger paste

- 2 tomatoes, chopped finely
- 1 tablespoon ground cumin
- 1 tablespoon ground coriander
- 1 teaspoon ground turmeric
- 1 teaspoon red chili powder
- Salt, to taste
- 1-pound lean ground chicken
- 2 cups frozen peas
- 1½ cups water
- 1-2 teaspoons garam masala powder

DIRECTIONS

1. In a deep skillet, heat oil on medium heat.
2. Add bay leaves and sauté for approximately half a minute.
3. Add onion paste and sauté for approximately 3-4 minutes.
4. Add garlic and ginger paste and sauté for around 1-1½ minutes.
5. Add tomatoes and spices and cook, stirring occasionally for about 3-4 minutes.
6. Stir in chicken and cook for about 4-5 minutes.
7. Stir in peas and water and bring to a boil on high heat.
8. Reduce the heat to low and simmer approximately 5-8 minutes or till desired doneness.
9. Stir in garam masala and remove from heat.
10. Serve hot.

NUTRITION: Calories: 450, Fat: 10g, Carbohydrates: 19g, Fiber: 6g, Protein: 38g

139. Chicken Meatballs Curry

Preparation Time: 20 min
Cooking Time: 25 minutes
Servings: 3-4
Difficulty: Medium
INGREDIENTS
For Meatballs:
- 1-pound lean ground chicken
- 1 tablespoon onion paste
- 1 teaspoon fresh ginger paste
- 1 teaspoons garlic paste
- 1 green chili, chopped finely
- 1 tablespoon fresh cilantro leaves, chopped
- 1 teaspoon ground coriander
- ½ teaspoon cumin seeds
- ½ teaspoon red chili powder
- ½ teaspoon ground turmeric
- Salt, to taste

For Curry:
- 3 tablespoons extra-virgin olive oil
- ½ teaspoon cumin seeds
- 1 (1-inch) cinnamon stick
- 3 whole cloves
- 3 whole green cardamoms
- 1 whole black cardamom
- 2 onions, chopped
- 1 teaspoon fresh ginger, minced
- 1 teaspoons garlic, minced
- 4 whole tomatoes, chopped finely
- 2 teaspoons ground coriander
- 1 teaspoon garam masala powder
- ½ teaspoon ground nutmeg
- ½ teaspoon red chili powder

- ½ teaspoon ground turmeric
- Salt, to taste
- 1 cup water
- Chopped fresh cilantro, for garnishing

DIRECTIONS

1. For meatballs in a substantial bowl, add all ingredients and mix till well combined.
2. Make small equal-sized meatballs from mixture.
3. In a big deep skillet, heat oil on medium heat.
4. Add meatballs and fry approximately 3-5 minutes or till browned from all sides.
5. Transfer the meatballs in a bowl.
6. In the same skillet, add cumin seeds, cinnamon stick, cloves, green cardamom and black cardamom and sauté approximately 1 minute.
7. Add onions and sauté for around 4-5 minutes.
8. Add ginger and garlic paste and sauté approximately 1 minute.
9. Add tomato and spices and cook, crushing with the back of spoon for approximately 2-3 minutes.
10. Add water and meatballs and provide to a boil.
11. Reduce heat to low.
12. Simmer for approximately 10 minutes.
13. Serve hot with all the garnishing of cilantro.

NUTRITION: Calories: 421, Fat: 8g, Carbohydrates: 18g, Fiber: 5g, Protein: 34g

140. Ground Chicken with Basil

Preparation Time: fifteen minutes
Cooking Time: 16 minutes
Servings: 8
Difficulty: Medium

INGREDIENTS

- 2 pounds lean ground chicken
- 3 tablespoons coconut oil, divided
- 1 zucchini, chopped
- 1 red bell pepper, seeded and chopped
- ½ of green bell pepper, seeded and chopped
- 4 garlic cloves, minced
- 1 (1-inch) piece fresh ginger, minced
- 1 (1-inch) piece fresh turmeric, minced
- 1 fresh red chile, sliced thinly
- 1 tablespoon organic honey
- 1 tablespoon coconut amino
- 1½ tablespoons fish sauce
- ½ cup fresh basil, chopped
- Salt and freshly ground black pepper, to taste
- 1 tablespoon fresh lime juice

DIRECTIONS

1. Heat a large skillet on medium-high heat.
2. Add ground beef and cook for approximately 5 minutes or till browned completely.
3. Transfer the beef in a bowl.
4. In a similar pan, melt 1 tablespoon of coconut oil on medium-high heat.

5. Add zucchini and bell peppers and stir fry for around 3-4 minutes.
6. Transfer the vegetables inside bowl with chicken.
7. In exactly the same pan, melt remaining coconut oil on medium heat.
8. Add garlic, ginger, turmeric and red chile and sauté for approximately 1-2 minutes.
9. Add chicken mixture, honey and coconut amino and increase the heat to high.
10. Cook, stirring occasionally for approximately 4-5 minutes or till sauce is nearly reduced.
11. Stir in remaining **ingredients** and take off from heat.

NUTRITION: Calories: 407, Fat: 7g, Carbohydrates: 20g, Fiber: 13g, Protein: 36g

141. Chicken &Veggie Casserole

Preparation Time: 15 minutes
Cooking Time: half an hour
Servings: 4
Difficulty: Medium
INGREDIENTS
- 1/3 cup Dijon mustard
- 1/3 cup organic honey
- 1 teaspoon dried basil
- ¼ teaspoon ground turmeric
- 1 teaspoon dried basil, crushed
- Salt and freshly ground black pepper, to taste
- 1¾ pound chicken breasts

- 1 cup fresh white mushrooms, sliced
- ½ head broccoli, cut into small florets

DIRECTIONS
1. Preheat the oven to 350 degrees F. Lightly, grease a baking dish.
2. In a bowl, mix together all ingredients except chicken, mushrooms and broccoli.
3. Arrange chicken in prepared baking dish and top with mushroom slices.
4. Place broccoli florets around chicken evenly.
5. Pour 1 / 2 of honey mixture over chicken and broccoli evenly.
6. Bake for approximately twenty minutes.
7. Now, coat the chicken with remaining sauce and bake for approximately 10 minutes.

NUTRITION: Calories: 427, Fat: 9g, Carbohydrates: 16g, Fiber: 7g, Protein: 35g

142. Chicken & Cauliflower Rice Casserole

Preparation Time: fifteen minutes
Cooking Time: an hour fifteen minutes
Servings: 8-10
Difficulty: hard
INGREDIENTS
- 2 tablespoons coconut oil, divided
- 3-pound bone-in chicken thighs and drumsticks
- Salt and freshly ground black pepper, to taste
- 3 carrots, peeled and sliced

- 1 onion, chopped finely
- 2 garlic cloves, chopped finely
- 2 tablespoons fresh cinnamon, chopped finely
- 2 teaspoons ground cumin
- 1 teaspoon ground coriander
- 12 teaspoon ground cinnamon
- ½ teaspoon ground turmeric
- 1 teaspoon paprika
- ¼ teaspoon red pepper cayenne
- 1 (28-ounce) can diced tomatoes with liquid
- 1 red bell pepper, seeded and cut into thin strips
- ½ cup fresh parsley leaves, minced
- Salt, to taste
- 1 head cauliflower, grated to some rice like consistency
- 1 lemon, sliced thinly

DIRECTIONS

1. Preheat the oven to 375 degrees F.
2. In a large pan, melt 1 tablespoon of coconut oil high heat.
3. Add chicken pieces and cook for about 3-5 minutes per side or till golden brown.
4. Transfer the chicken in a plate.
5. In a similar pan, sauté the carrot, onion, garlic and ginger for about 4-5 minutes on medium heat.
6. Stir in spices and remaining coconut oil.
7. Add chicken, tomatoes, bell pepper, parsley and salt and simmer for approximately 3-5 minutes.
8. In the bottom of a 13x9-inch rectangular baking dish, spread the cauliflower rice evenly.
9. Place chicken mixture over cauliflower rice evenly and top with lemon slices.
10. With a foil paper, cover the baking dish and bake for approximately 35 minutes.
11. Uncover the baking dish and bake approximately 25 minutes.

NUTRITION: Calories: 412, Fat: 12g, Carbohydrates: 23g, Fiber: 7g, Protein: 34g

143. Chicken Meatloaf with Veggies

Preparation Time: 20 minutes
Cooking Time: 1-1¼ hours
Servings: 4
Difficulty: hard
INGREDIENTS
For Meatloaf:
- ½ cup cooked chickpeas
- 2 egg whites
- 2½ teaspoons poultry seasoning
- Salt and freshly ground black pepper, to taste
- 10-ounce lean ground chicken
- 1 cup red bell pepper, seeded and minced
- 1 cup celery stalk, minced
- 1/3 cup steel-cut oats
- 1 cup tomato puree, divided
- 2 tablespoons dried onion flakes, crushed
- 1 tablespoon prepared mustard

For Veggies:

- 2-pounds summer squash, sliced
- 16-ounce frozen Brussels sprouts
- 2 tablespoons extra-virgin extra virgin olive oil
- Salt and freshly ground black pepper, to taste

DIRECTIONS

1. Preheat the oven to 350 degrees F. Grease a 9x5-inch loaf pan.
2. In a mixer, add chickpeas, egg whites, poultry seasoning, salt and black pepper and pulse till smooth.
3. Transfer a combination in a large bowl.
4. Add chicken, veggies oats, ½ cup of tomato puree and onion flakes and mix till well combined.
5. Transfer the amalgamation into prepared loaf pan evenly.
6. With both hands, press, down the amalgamation slightly.
7. In another bowl mix together mustard and remaining tomato puree.
8. Place the mustard mixture over loaf pan evenly.
9. Bake approximately 1-1¼ hours or till desired doneness.
10. Meanwhile in a big pan of water, arrange a steamer basket.
11. Bring to a boil and set summer time squash in steamer basket.
12. Cover and steam approximately 10-12 minutes.
13. Drain well and aside.
14. Now, prepare the Brussels sprouts according to package's **directions**.
15. In a big bowl, add veggies, oil, salt and black pepper and toss to coat well.
16. Serve the meatloaf with veggies.

NUTRITION: Calories: 420, Fat: 9g, Carbohydrates: 21g, Fiber: 14g, Protein: 36g

144. Roasted Spatchcock Chicken

Preparation Time: twenty or so minutes
Cooking Time: 50 minutes
Servings: 4-6
Difficulty: hard

INGREDIENTS

- 1 (4-pound) whole chicken
- 1 (1-inch) piece fresh ginger, sliced
- 4 garlic cloves, chopped
- 1 small bunch fresh thyme
- Pinch of cayenne
- Salt and freshly ground black pepper, to taste
- ¼ cup fresh lemon juice
- 3 tablespoons extra virgin olive oil

DIRECTIONS

1. Arrange chicken, breast side down onto a large cutting board.
2. With a kitchen shear, begin with thigh and cut along 1 side of backbone and turn chicken around.
3. Now, cut along sleep issues and discard the backbone.
4. Change the inside and open it like a book.

5. Flatten the backbone firmly to flatten.
6. In a food processor, add all ingredients except chicken and pulse till smooth.
7. In a big baking dish, add the marinade mixture.
8. Add chicken and coat with marinade generously.
9. With a plastic wrap, cover the baking dish and refrigerate to marinate for overnight.
10. Preheat the oven to 450 degrees F. Arrange a rack in a very roasting pan.
11. Remove the chicken from refrigerator make onto rack over roasting pan, skin side down.
12. Roast for about 50 minutes, turning once in the middle way.

NUTRITION: Calories: 419, Fat: 14g, Carbohydrates: 28g, Fiber: 4g, Protein: 40g

145. Creamy Mushroom and Broccoli Chicken

Preparation Time: 15 minutes

Cooking Time: 6 hours
Servings: 6
Difficulty: hard
INGREDIENTS

- 1 10.5 ounce can of low-sodium cream of mushroom soup
- 1 21 ounce can of low-sodium cream of Chicken Soup
- 2 whole cooked chicken breasts, chopped or shredded
- 2 cup milk
- 1lb broccoli florets
- ¼ teaspoon garlic powder

DIRECTIONS

1. Place all ingredients to a 5 quart or larger slow cooker and mix well.
2. Cover and cook on LOW for 6 hours.
3. Serve with potatoes, pasta, or rice.

NUTRITION: Calories 155, Fat 2g, Carbs 19g, Protein 12g, Fiber 2g, Potassium 755mg, Sodium 35mg

DESSERTS

146. Dessert Cocktail

Preparation Time: 1 minutes
Cooking Time: 0 minute
Servings: 4
Difficulty: Easy

INGREDIENTS

- 1 cup of cranberry juice
- 1 cup of fresh ripe strawberries, washed and hull removed
- 2 tablespoon of lime juice
- ¼ cup of white sugar
- 8 ice cubes

DIRECTIONS

1. Combine all the ingredients in a blender until smooth and creamy.
2. Pour the liquid into chilled tall glasses and serve cold.

NUTRITION: Calories: 92 kcal Carbohydrate: 23.5 g Protein: 0.5 g Sodium: 3.62 mg Potassium: 103.78 mg Phosphorus: 17.86 mg Dietary Fiber: 0.84 g Fat: 0.17 g

147. Baked Egg Custard

Preparation Time: 15 minutes
Cooking Time: 30 minutes
Servings: 4
Difficulty: Easy

INGREDIENTS

- 2 medium eggs, at room temperature
- ¼ cup of semi-skimmed milk
- 3 tablespoons of white sugar
- ½ teaspoon of nutmeg
- 1 teaspoon of vanilla extract

DIRECTIONS

1. Preheat your oven at 375 F/180C
2. Mix all the ingredients in a mixing bowl and beat with a hand mixer for a few seconds until creamy and uniform.
3. Pour the mixture into lightly greased muffin tins.
4. Bake for 25-30 minutes or until the knife, you place inside, comes out clean.

NUTRITION: Calories: 96.56 kcal Carbohydrate: 10.5 g Protein: 3.5 g Sodium: 37.75 mg Potassium: 58.19 mg Phosphorus: 58.76 mg Dietary Fiber: 0.06 g Fat: 2.91 g

148. Apple Crunch Pie

Preparation Time: 10 minutes
Cooking Time: 35 minutes
Servings: 8
Difficulty: Easy
INGREDIENTS

- 4 large tart apples, peeled, seeded and sliced
- ½ cup of white all-purpose flour
- ⅓ cup margarine
- 1 cup of sugar
- ¾ cup of rolled oat flakes
- ½ teaspoon of ground nutmeg

DIRECTIONS

1. Preheat the oven to 375F/180C.
2. Place the apples over a lightly greased square pan (around 7 inches).
3. Mix the rest of the ingredients in a medium bowl with and spread the batter over the apples.
4. Bake for 30-35 minutes or until the top crust has gotten golden brown.
5. Serve hot.

NUTRITION: Calories: 261.9 kcal Carbohydrate: 47.2 g Protein: 1.5 g Sodium: 81 mg Potassium: 123.74 mg Phosphorus: 35.27 mg Dietary Fiber: 2.81 g Fat: 7.99 g

149. Pound Cake with Pineapple

Preparation Time: 10 minutes
Cooking Time: 50 minutes
Servings: 24
Difficulty: Easy
INGREDIENTS

- 3 cups of all-purpose flour, sifted
- 3 cups of sugar
- 1 ½ cups of butter
- 6 whole eggs and 3 egg whites
- 1 teaspoon of vanilla extract
- 1 10. Ounce can of pineapple chunks, rinsed and crushed (keep juice aside).

For glaze:

- 1 cup of sugar
- 1 stick of unsalted butter or margarine
- Reserved juice from the pineapple

DIRECTIONS

1. Preheat the oven at 350F/180C.
2. Beat the sugar and the butter with a hand mixer until creamy and smooth.
3. Slowly add the eggs (one or two every time) and stir well after pouring each egg.
4. Add the vanilla extract, follow up with the flour and stir well.
5. Add the drained and chopped pineapple.
6. Pour the mixture into a greased cake tin and bake for 45-50 minutes.

7. In a small saucepan, combine the sugar with the butter and pineapple juice. Stir every few seconds and bring to boil. Cook until you get a creamy to thick glaze consistency.
8. Pour the glaze over the cake while still hot.
9. Let cook for at least 10 seconds and serve.

NUTRITION: Calories: 407.4 kcal Carbohydrate: 79 g Protein: 4.25 g Sodium: 118.97 mg Potassium: 180.32 mg Phosphorus: 66.37 mg Dietary Fiber: 2.25 g Fat: 16.48 g

150. Gumdrop Cookies

Preparation Time: 15 minutes
Cooking Time: 12 minutes
Servings: 25
Difficulty: Easy
INGREDIENTS
- ½ cup of spreadable unsalted butter
- 1 medium egg
- 1 cup of brown sugar
- 1 ⅔ cups of all-purpose flour, sifted
- ¼ cup of milk
- 1 teaspoon vanilla
- 1 teaspoon of baking powder
- 15 large gumdrops, chopped finely

DIRECTIONS
1. Preheat the oven at 400F/195C.
2. Combine the sugar, butter and egg until creamy.
3. Add the milk and vanilla and stir well.

4. Combine the flour with the baking powder in a different bowl. Incorporate to the sugar, butter mixture, and stir.
5. Add the gumdrops and place the mixture in the fridge for half an hour.
6. Drop the dough with tablespoonful into a lightly greased baking or cookie sheet.
7. Bake for 10-12 minutes or until golden brown in color.

NUTRITION: Calories: 102.17 kcal Carbohydrate: 16.5 g Protein: 0.86 g Sodium: 23.42 mg Potassium: 45 mg Phosphorus: 32.15 mg Dietary Fiber: 0.13 g Fat: 4 g

151. Spiced Peaches

Preparation Time: 5 minutes
Cooking Time: 10 minutes
Servings: 2
Difficulty: Easy
INGREDIENTS
- Canned peaches with juices – 1 cup
- Cornstarch – ½ teaspoon
- Ground cloves – 1 teaspoon
- Ground cinnamon – 1 teaspoon
- Ground nutmeg – 1 teaspoon
- Zest of ½ lemon
- Water – ½ cup

DIRECTIONS
1. Drain peaches.
2. Combine cinnamon, cornstarch, nutmeg, ground cloves, and lemon zest in a pan on the stove.

3. Heat on a medium heat and add peaches.
4. Bring to a boil, reduce the heat and simmer for 10 minutes.
5. Serve.

NUTRITION: Calories: 70 Fat: 0g Carb: 14g Phosphorus: 23mg Potassium: 176mg Sodium: 3mg Protein: 1g

152. Pumpkin Cheesecake Bar

Preparation Time: 10 minutes
Cooking Time: 50 minutes
Servings: 4
Difficulty: Easy
INGREDIENTS
- Unsalted butter – 2 ½ Tablespoons.
- Cream cheese – 4 ounces
- All-purpose white flour – ½ cup
- Golden brown sugar – 3 Tablespoons.
- Granulated sugar – ¼ cup
- Pureed pumpkin – ½ cup
- Egg whites - 2
- Ground cinnamon – 1 teaspoon
- Ground nutmeg – 1 teaspoon
- Vanilla extract – 1 teaspoon

DIRECTIONS
1. Preheat the oven to 350F.
2. Mix flour and brown sugar in a bowl.
3. Mix in the butter to form 'breadcrumbs.
4. Place ¾ of this mixture in a dish.
5. Bake in the oven for 15 minutes. Remove and cool.

6. Lightly whisk the egg and fold in the cream cheese, sugar, pumpkin, cinnamon, nutmeg and vanilla until smooth.
7. Pour this mixture over the oven-baked base and sprinkle with the rest of the breadcrumbs from earlier.
8. Bake in the oven for 30 to 35 minutes more.
9. Cool, slice and serve.

NUTRITION: Calories: 248 Fat: 13g Carb: 33g Phosphorus: 67mg Potassium: 96mg Sodium: 146mg Protein: 4g

153. Blueberry Mini Muffins

Preparation Time: 10 minutes
Cooking Time: 35 minutes
Servings: 4
Difficulty: Easy
INGREDIENTS
- Egg whites – 3
- All-purpose white flour – ¼ cup
- Coconut flour – 1 Tablespoon
- Baking soda – 1 teaspoon
- Nutmeg – 1 Tablespoon grated
- Vanilla extract – 1 teaspoon
- Stevia – 1 teaspoon
- Fresh blueberries – ¼ cup

DIRECTIONS
1. Preheat the oven to 325F.
2. Mix all the ingredients in a bowl.
3. Divide the batter into 4 and spoon into a lightly oiled muffin tin.
4. Bake in the oven for 15 to 20 minutes or until cooked through.
5. Cool and serve.

NUTRITION: Calories: 62 Fat: 0g Carb: 9g Phosphorus: 103mg Potassium: 65mg Sodium: 62mg Protein: 4g

154. Vanilla Custard

Preparation Time: 7 minutes
Cooking Time: 10 minutes
Servings: 10
Difficulty: Easy
INGREDIENTS

- Egg – 1
- Vanilla – 1/8 teaspoon
- Nutmeg – 1/8 teaspoon
- Almond milk – ½ cup
- Stevia - 2 Tablespoon

DIRECTIONS

1. Scald the milk then let it cool slightly.
2. Break the egg into a bowl and beat it with the nutmeg.
3. Add the scalded milk, the vanilla, and the sweetener to taste. Mix well.
4. Place the bowl in a baking pan filled with ½ deep of water.
5. Bake for 30 minutes at 325F.
6. Serve.

NUTRITION: Calories: 167.3 Fat: 9g Carb: 11g Phosphorus: 205mg Potassium: 249mg Sodium: 124mg Protein: 10g

155. Chocolate Chip Cookies

Preparation Time: 7 minutes
Cooking Time: 10 minutes
Servings: 10
Difficulty: Easy
INGREDIENTS

- Semi-sweet chocolate chips – ½ cup
- Baking soda – ½ teaspoon
- Vanilla – ½ teaspoon
- Egg – 1
- Flour – 1 cup
- Margarine – ½ cup
- Stevia – 4 teaspoons

DIRECTIONS

1. Sift the dry **ingredients**.
2. Cream the margarine, stevia, vanilla and egg with a whisk.
3. Add flour mixture and beat well.
4. Stir in the chocolate chips, then drop teaspoonful of the mixture over a greased baking sheet.
5. Bake the cookies for about 10 minutes at 375F.
6. Cool and serve.

NUTRITION: Calories: 106.2 Fat: 7g Carb: 8.9g Phosphorus: 19mg Potassium: 28mg Sodium: 98mg Protein: 1.5g

156. Lemon Mousse

Preparation Time: 10 + chill time
Cooking Time: 10 minutes
Servings: 4
Difficulty: Easy
INGREDIENTS

- 1 cup coconut cream
- 8 ounces cream cheese, soft
- ¼ cup fresh lemon juice
- 3 pinches salt
- 1 teaspoon lemon liquid stevia

DIRECTIONS

1. Preheat your oven to 350 °F
2. Grease a ramekin with butter

3. Beat cream, cream cheese, fresh lemon juice, salt and lemon liquid stevia in a mixer
4. Pour batter into ramekin
5. Bake for 10 minutes, then transfer the mousse to a serving glass
6. Let it chill for 2 hours and serve
7. Enjoy!

NUTRITION: Calories: 395 Fat: 31g Carbohydrates: 3g Protein: 5g

157. Jalapeno Crisp

Preparation Time: 10 minutes
Cooking Time: 1 hour 15 minutes
Servings: 20
Difficulty: Easy
INGREDIENTS
- 1 cup sesame seeds
- 1 cup sunflower seeds
- 1 cup flaxseeds
- ½ cup hulled hemp seeds
- 3 tablespoons Psyllium husk
- 1 teaspoon salt
- 1 teaspoon baking powder
- 2 cups of water

DIRECTIONS
1. Pre-heat your oven to 350 °F
2. Take your blender and add seeds, baking powder, salt, and Psyllium husk
3. Blend well until a sand-like texture appears
4. Stir in water and mix until a batter form

5. Allow the batter to rest for 10 minutes until a dough-like thick mixture forms
6. Pour the dough onto a cookie sheet lined with parchment paper
7. Spread it evenly, making sure that it has a thickness of ¼ inch thick all around
8. Bake for 75 minutes in your oven
9. Remove and cut into 20 spices
10. Allow them to cool for 30 minutes and enjoy!

NUTRITION: Calories: 156 Fat: 13g Carbohydrates: 2g Protein: 5g

158. Raspberry Popsicle

Preparation Time: 2 hours
Cooking Time: 15 minutes
Servings: 4
Difficulty: Easy
INGREDIENTS
- 1 ½ cups raspberries
- 2 cups of water

DIRECTIONS
1. Take a pan and fill it up with water
2. Add raspberries
3. Place it over medium heat and bring to water to a boil
4. Reduce the heat and simmer for 15 minutes
5. Remove heat and pour the mix into Popsicle molds
6. Add a popsicle stick and let it chill for 2 hours
7. Serve and enjoy!

NUTRITION: Calories: 58 Fat: 0.4g Carbohydrates: 0g Protein: 1.4g

159. Easy Fudge

Preparation Time: 15 minutes + chill time
Cooking Time: 5 minutes
Servings: 25
Difficulty: Easy
INGREDIENTS

- 1 ¾ cups of coconut butter
- 1 cup pumpkin puree
- 1 teaspoon ground cinnamon
- ¼ teaspoon ground nutmeg
- 1 tablespoon coconut oil

DIRECTIONS

1. Take an 8x8 inch square baking pan and line it with aluminum foil
2. Take a spoon and scoop out the coconut butter into a heated pan and allow the butter to melt
3. Keep stirring well and remove from the heat once fully melted
4. Add spices and pumpkin and keep straining until you have a grain-like texture
5. Add coconut oil and keep stirring to incorporate everything
6. Scoop the mixture into your baking pan and evenly distribute it
7. Place wax paper on top of the mixture and press gently to straighten the top
8. Remove the paper and discard
9. Allow it to chill for 1-2 hours
10. Once chilled, take it out and slice it up into pieces

11. Enjoy!

NUTRITION: Calories: 120 Fat: 10g Carbohydrates: 5g Protein: 1.2g

160. Coconut Loaf

Preparation Time: 15 minutes
Cooking Time: 40 minutes
Servings: 4
Difficulty: Easy
INGREDIENTS

- 1 ½ tablespoons coconut flour
- ¼ teaspoon baking powder
- 1/8 teaspoon salt
- 1 tablespoon coconut oil, melted
- 1 whole egg

DIRECTIONS

1. Preheat your oven to 350 °F
2. Add coconut flour, baking powder, salt
3. Add coconut oil, eggs and stir well until mixed
4. Leave the batter for several minutes
5. Pour half the batter onto the baking pan
6. Spread it to form a circle, repeat with remaining batter
7. Bake in the oven for 10 minutes
8. Once a golden-brown texture comes, let it cool and serve
9. Enjoy!

NUTRITION: Calories: 297 Fat: 14g Carbohydrates: 15g Protein: 15g

161. Chocolate Parfait

Preparation Time: 2 hours

Cooking Time: 0 minute
Servings: 4
Difficulty: Easy
INGREDIENTS

- Take a bowl and add cocoa powder, almond milk, chia seeds, vanilla extract, and stir
- Transfer to dessert glass and place in your fridge for 2 hours
- Serve and enjoy!

DIRECTIONS

1. Take a bowl and add cocoa powder, almond milk, chia seeds, vanilla extract, and stir
2. Transfer to dessert glass and place in your fridge for 2 hours
3. Serve and enjoy!

NUTRITION: Calories: 130 Fat: 5g Carbohydrates: 7g Protein: 16g

162. Cauliflower Bagel

Preparation Time: 10 minutes
Cooking Time: 30 minutes
Servings: 12
Difficulty: Easy
INGREDIENTS

- 1 large cauliflower, divided into florets and roughly chopped
- ¼ cup **nutrition**al yeast
- ¼ cup almond flour
- ½ teaspoon garlic powder
- 1 ½ teaspoon fine sea salt
- 2 whole eggs
- 1 tablespoon sesame seeds

DIRECTIONS

1. Preheat your oven to 400 °F

2. Line a baking sheet with parchment paper, keep it on the side
3. Blend cauliflower in a food processor and transfer to a bowl
4. Add **nutrition**al yeast, almond flour, garlic powder and salt to a bowl, mix
5. Take another bowl and whisk in eggs, add to cauliflower mix
6. Give the dough a stir
7. Incorporate the mix into the egg mix
8. Make balls from the dough, making a hole using your thumb into each ball
9. Arrange them on your prepped sheet, flattening them into bagel shapes
10. Sprinkle sesame seeds and bake for half an hour
11. Remove the oven and let them cool, enjoy!

NUTRITION: Calories: 152 Fat: 10g Carbohydrates: 4g Protein: 4g

163. Almond Crackers

Preparation Time: 10 minutes
Cooking Time: 20 minutes
Servings: 40 crackers
Difficulty: Easy
INGREDIENTS

- 1 cup almond flour
- ¼ teaspoon baking soda
- ¼ teaspoon salt
- 1/8 teaspoon black pepper
- 3 tablespoons sesame seeds
- 1 egg, beaten
- Salt and pepper to taste

DIRECTIONS

1. Preheat your oven to 350 °F
2. Line two baking sheets with parchment paper and keep them on the side
3. Mix the dry **ingredients** into a large bowl and add egg, mix well and form a dough
4. Divide dough into two balls
5. Roll out the dough between two pieces of parchment paper
6. Cut into crackers and transfer them to prep a baking sheet
7. Bake for 15-20 minutes
8. Repeat until all the dough has been used up
9. Leave crackers to cool and serve
10. Enjoy!

NUTRITION: Calories: 302 Fat: 28g Carbohydrates: 4g Protein: 9g

164. Cashew and Almond Butter

Preparation Time: 5 minutes
Cooking Time: 15 minutes
Servings: 1 ½ cups
Difficulty: Easy
INGREDIENTS
- 1 cup almonds, blanched
- 1/3 cup cashew nuts
- 2 tablespoons coconut oil
- Salt as needed
- ½ teaspoon cinnamon

DIRECTIONS
1. Preheat your oven to 350 °F
2. Bake almonds and cashews for 12 minutes

3. Let them cool
4. Transfer to a food processor and add remaining **ingredients**
5. Add oil and keep blending until smooth
6. Serve and enjoy!

NUTRITION: Calories: 205 Fat: 19g Carbohydrates: g Protein: 2.8g

165. Nut and Chia Mix

Preparation Time: 10 minutes
Cooking Time: 0 minute
Servings: 1
Difficulty: Easy
INGREDIENTS
- 1 tablespoon chia seeds
- 2 cups of water
- 1-ounce Macadamia nuts
- 1-2 packets Stevia, optional
- 1-ounce hazelnuts

DIRECTIONS
1. Add all the listed **ingredients** to a blender.
2. Blend on high until smooth and creamy.
3. Enjoy your smoothie.

NUTRITION: Calories: 452 Fat: 43g Carbohydrates: 15g Protein: 9g

166. Hearty Cucumber Bites

Preparation Time: 5 minutes
Cooking Time: 0 minute
Servings: 4
Difficulty: Easy
INGREDIENTS

- 1 (8 ounces) cream cheese container, low fat
- 1 tablespoon bell pepper, diced
- 1 tablespoon shallots, diced
- 1 tablespoon parsley, chopped
- 2 cucumbers
- Pepper to taste

DIRECTIONS

1. Take a bowl and add cream cheese, onion, pepper, parsley
2. Peel cucumbers and cut in half
3. Remove seeds and stuff with the cheese mix
4. Cut into bite-sized portions and enjoy!

NUTRITION: Calories: 85 Fat: 4g Carbohydrates: 2g Protein: 3g

167. Hearty Almond Bread

Preparation Time: 15 minutes
Cooking Time: 60 minutes
Servings: 8
Difficulty: Easy
INGREDIENTS

- 3 cups almond flour
- 1 teaspoon baking soda
- 2 teaspoons baking powder
- ¼ teaspoon sunflower seeds
- ¼ cup almond milk
- ½ cup + 2 tablespoons olive oil
- 3 whole eggs

DIRECTIONS

1. Preheat your oven to 300 ° F
2. Take a 9x5 inch loaf pan and grease, keep it on the side

3. Add the listed **ingredients** to a bowl and pour the batter into the loaf pan
4. Bake for 60 minutes
5. Once baked, remove from oven and let it cool
6. Slice and serve!

NUTRITION: Calories: 277 Fat: 21g Carbohydrates: 7g Protein: 10g

168. Medjool Balls

Preparation Time: 5 minutes + 20 minutes chill time
Cooking Time: 2-3 minutes
Servings: 4
Difficulty: Easy
INGREDIENTS

- 3 cups Medjool dates, chopped
- 12 ounces brewed coffee
- 1 cup pecan, chopped
- ½ cup coconut, shredded
- ½ cup of cocoa powder

DIRECTIONS

1. Soak dates in warm coffee for 5 minutes
2. Remove dates from coffee and mash them, making a fine smooth mixture
3. Stir in remaining **ingredients** (except cocoa powder) and form small balls out of the mixture
4. Coat with cocoa powder, serve and enjoy!

NUTRITION: Calories: 265 Fat: 12g Carbohydrates: 43g Protein 3g

169. Blueberry Pudding

Preparation Time: 20 minutes
Cooking Time: 0 minute
Servings: 4
Difficulty: Easy
INGREDIENTS

- 2 cups of frozen blueberries
- 2 teaspoon of lime zest, grated freshly
- 20 drops of liquid stevia
- ½ teaspoon of fresh ginger, grated freshly
- 4 tablespoon of fresh lime juice
- 10 tablespoons of water

DIRECTIONS

1. Add all of the listed **ingredients** to a blender (except blueberries) and pulse the mixture well
2. Transfer the mix into small serving bowls and chill the bowls
3. Serve with a topping of blueberries
4. Enjoy!

NUTRITION: Calories: 166 Fat: 13g Carbohydrates: 13g Protein: 1.7g

170. Chia Seed Pumpkin Pudding

Preparation Time: 10-15 minutes/ overnight chill time
Cooking Time: 0 minute
Servings: 4
Difficulty: Easy
INGREDIENTS

- 1 cup maple syrup
- 2 teaspoons pumpkin spice

- 1 cup pumpkin puree
- 1 ¼ cup of almond milk
- ½ cup chia seeds

DIRECTIONS

1. Add all of the ingredients to a bowl and gently stir
2. Let it refrigerate overnight or for at least 15 minutes
3. Top with your desired **ingredients** such as blueberries, almonds, etcetera.
4. Serve and enjoy!

NUTRITION: Calories: 230 Fat: 10g Carbohydrates: 22g Protein: 11g

171. Parsley Souffle

Preparation Time: 5 minutes
Cooking Time: 6 minutes
Servings: 5
Difficulty: Easy
INGREDIENTS

- 2 whole eggs
- 1 fresh red chili pepper, chopped
- 2 tablespoons coconut cream
- 1 tablespoon fresh parsley, chopped
- Sunflower seeds to taste

DIRECTIONS

1. Preheat your oven to 390 °F
2. Almond butter two soufflé dishes
3. Add the ingredients to a blender and mix well
4. Divide batter into soufflé dishes and bake for 6 minutes
5. Serve and enjoy!

NUTRITION: Calories: 108 Fat: 9g Carbohydrates: 9g Protein: 6g

172. Crunchy Banana Cookies

Preparation Time: 15 minutes
Cooking Time: 15 minutes
Servings: 30
Difficulty: Easy
INGREDIENTS

- 1/2 cup unsalted butter (1 stick), room temperature
- 1 cup sugar
- 1 egg, room temperature
- 1 cup mashed bananas (about 2 ½ large bananas)
- 1 teaspoon baking soda
- 2 cups all-purpose flour
- pinch salt
- 1/2 teaspoon ground cinnamon
- 1/2 teaspoon ground mace or nutmeg
- 1/2 teaspoon ground cloves
- 1 cup pecans (walnuts and chocolate chips are fine alternatives)

DIRECTIONS

1. Preheat the oven to 350°F. Beat the butter and sugar together until light and fluffy. Add the egg and continue to beat until the mixture is light and fluffy.
2. In a separate bowl, mix the mashed bananas and baking soda. Let sit for 2 minutes. The baking soda will react with the acid in the bananas which in turn will give the cookies their lift and rise.
3. Mix the banana mixture into the butter mixture.
4. Whisk together the flour, salt, and spices. Add to the butter and banana mixture and mix until just combined.
5. Fold pecans or chocolate chips (if using) into the batter.
6. Drop in dollops onto parchment paper-lined baking sheet. Bake for 11-13 minutes or until nicely golden brown. Let cool on wire racks.

NUTRITION: Calories: 64.7 kcal Total Fat: 1.8 g Saturated Fat: 0.9 g Cholesterol: 0.2 mg Sodium: 0.9 mg Total Carbs: 12.2 g Fiber: 1.2 g Sugar: 0.2 g Protein: 1.2 g

173. Fluffy Mock Pancakes

Preparation Time: 5 minutes
Cooking Time: 10 minutes
Servings: 2
Difficulty: Easy
INGREDIENTS

- 1 egg
- 1 cup ricotta cheese
- 1 teaspoon cinnamon
- 2 tablespoons honey, add more if needed

DIRECTIONS

1. Using a blender, put together egg, honey, cinnamon, and ricotta cheese. Process until all ingredients are well combined.
2. Pour an equal amount of the blended mixture into the pan. Cook each pancake for 4 minutes on both sides. Serve.

NUTRITION: Calories: 188.1 kcal Total Fat: 14.5 g Saturated Fat: 4.5 g Cholesterol: 139.5 mg Sodium: 175.5 mg Total Carbs: 5.5 g Fiber: 2.8 g Sugar: 0.9 g Protein: 8.5 g

174. Baked Zucchini Chips

Preparation Time: 10 minutes
Cooking Time: 1 hour 30 minutes
Servings: 4
Difficulty: Easy
INGREDIENTS
- Cooking spray
- 2 zucchinis, sliced very thinly into coins
- 1 tablespoon extra-virgin olive oil (for baked version only)
- 1 tablespoon ranch seasoning
- 1 teaspoon dried oregano
- Kosher salt
- Freshly ground black pepper

DIRECTIONS
FOR OVEN

1. Preheat oven to 225°. Grease a large baking sheet with cooking spray. Slice zucchini into very thin rounds, using a mandolin if you have one! Pat zucchini with paper towels to draw out excess moisture.
2. In a large bowl, toss zucchini with oil then toss in ranch seasoning, oregano, salt, and pepper. Place in a single layer on baking sheets.
3. Bake until crispy, about 1 hour 20 minutes, checking after about an hour. Let cool to room temperature before serving.

FOR AIR FRYER

1. Grease air fryer basket lightly with cooking spray. Slice zucchini into very thin rounds, using a mandolin if you have one! Pat zucchini with paper towels to draw out excess moisture.
2. Omit oil. In a large bowl, toss zucchini with ranch seasoning, oregano, salt, and pepper. Place in a single layer in basket (a little overlapping is fine!).
3. Air fry at 375° for 6 minutes, then flip and cook for another 6 minutes. Remove golden chips and continue cooking remaining chips until golden and crispy, 2 to 4 minutes, shaking basket every minute to allow for even crisping.

NUTRITION: Calories: 15.2 kcal Total Fat: 0.1 g Saturated Fat: 0 g Cholesterol: 0 mg Sodium: 77.3 mg Total Carbs: 3.6 g Fiber: 1.3 g Sugar: 1.5 g Protein: 0.6 g

175. Mixes of Snack

Preparation Time: 10 minutes
Cooking Time: 1 hours and 15 minutes
Servings: 4
Difficulty: Easy
INGREDIENTS

- 6 cup margarine
- 2 tablespoon Worcestershire sauce
- 1 ½ tablespoon spice salt
- ¾ cup garlic powder
- ½ teaspoon onion powder
- 3 cups Crispi
- 3 cups Cheerios
- 3 cups corn flakes
- 1 cup KIXE
- 1 cup pretzels
- 1 cup broken bagel chips into 1-inch pieces

DIRECTIONS

1. Preheat the oven to 250F (120C)
2. Melt the margarine in a large roasting pan. Stir in the seasoning. Gradually add the ingredients remaining by mixing so that the coating is uniform.
3. Cook 1 hour, stirring every 15 minutes. Spread on paper towels to let cool. Store in a tightly-closed container.

NUTRITION: Calories: 200 kcal Total Fat: 9 g Saturated Fat: 3.5 g   Cholesterol: 0 mg Sodium: 3.5 mg Total Carbs: 27 g Fiber: 2 g Sugar: 0 g   Protein: 3 g

176. Parmesan Crisps

Preparation Time: 10 minutes
Cooking Time: 8 minutes
Servings: 4
Difficulty: Easy
INGREDIENTS

- 2 ounces grated fresh Parmesan cheese (about 1/2 cup)
- 1/4 teaspoon freshly ground black pepper

DIRECTIONS

1. Preheat oven to 400°.
2. Line a large baking sheet with parchment paper. Spoon cheese by tablespoonful 2 inches apart on prepared baking sheet. Spread each mound to a 2-inch diameter. Sprinkle mounds with pepper. Bake at 400° for 6 to 8 minutes or until crisp and golden. Cool completely on baking sheet. Remove from baking sheet using a thin spatula.
3. Kids Can Help: Let kids sprinkle the grated cheese onto the baking sheets.

NUTRITION: Calories: 31 kcal Total Fat: 2 g Saturated Fat: 1.2 g   Cholesterol: 6 mg Sodium: 108 mg Total Carbs: 0.3 g Fiber: 0 g Sugar: 0 g   Protein: 3 g

177. Crispy Tomato Chips

Preparation Time: 20 minutes
Cooking Time: 8 minutes
Servings: 2
Difficulty: Easy

INGREDIENTS

- 2 large firm tomatoes, sliced thinly (about 1/16th of an inch)
- kosher salt
- cooking spray

DIRECTIONS

1. Lay sliced tomatoes on a cutting board.
2. Sprinkle generously with salt, let sit for 15 minutes.
3. Pat the tomatoes with a paper towel to soak up the moisture.
4. Flip the tomatoes, re-salt and let sit for another 5 minutes.
5. Repeat the process with the paper towel.
6. Spray a flat, microwaveable plate with cooking spray (I used olive oil spray)
7. Arrange the tomato slices on the plate and spray them with cooking spray.
8. Microwave for 5 minutes on power level 7. (see note)
9. Remove the plate from the microwave, carefully flip the tomatoes and microwave for another minute.
10. Remove from the microwave, transfer the tomatoes which should be mostly dry and crisp at this point to a cooling rack.
11. Notes
12. *My microwave has 10 power levels. I reduced it to 7 from 10 for this. If you can't adjust your power levels, just check the tomatoes during the initial 5 minutes. They should be starting to dry and stiffen by the end of the time period. It might be shorter or longer depending on your microwave.

NUTRITION: Calories: 32.7 kcal Total Fat: 1.3 g Saturated Fat: 0.8 g Cholesterol: 4.1 mg Sodium: 76.7 mg Total Carbs: 3.6 g Fiber: 0.9 g Sugar: 0 g Protein: 2.3 g

178. Easy Ham and Dill Pickle Bites

Preparation Time: 10 minutes
Cooking Time: 35 minutes
Servings: 6
Difficulty: Easy

INGREDIENTS

- dill pickle
- cream cheese
- thinly sliced ham

DIRECTIONS

1. Let the cream cheese sit at room temperature for at least 30 minutes before you make these.
2. Cut dill pickles lengthwise into fourths or sixths, depending on how thick the pickles are. You need as many cut pickles spears as you have ham slices.
3. Spread each slice of ham with a very thin layer of cream cheese. (I used about 1 teaspoons cream cheese on each ham slice. The ham doesn't need to be completely covered with cream cheese.).

4. Put a dill pickle on the edge of each ham slice and trim the ham if it's very much bigger than the dill pickle spear. Roll up the ham around the dill pickle, then place toothpicks where you want each piece to be cut. Cut into pieces so that each piece has a toothpick. Arrange on plate and serve.

NUTRITION: Calories: 46.6 kcal Total Fat: 3.1 g Saturated Fat: 1.8 g Cholesterol: 12.4 mg   Sodium: 584.5 mg Total Carbs: 1.6 g Fiber: 0.4 g Sugar: 1.3 g Protein: 2.6 g

179. Tasty Salmon Sandwich

Preparation Time: 10 minutes
Cooking Time: 0 minute
Servings: 2
Difficulty: Easy
INGREDIENTS
- 3 ounces cream cheese, softened
- 1 tablespoon mayonnaise
- 1 tablespoon lemon juice
- 1 teaspoon dill weed
- 1/4 to 1/2 teaspoon salt
- 1/8 teaspoon pepper
- 1 can (6 ounces) pink salmon, drained, bones and skin removed
- 1/2 cup shredded carrot
- 1/2 cup chopped celery
- Lettuce leaves
- 2 whole wheat buns, split

DIRECTIONS
1. In a large bowl, beat the cream cheese, mayonnaise, lemon juice, dill, salt and pepper until smooth. Add

the salmon, carrot and celery and mix well. Place a lettuce leaf and about 1/2 cup salmon salad on each bun.

NUTRITION: Calories: 463 kcal Total Fat: 29 g Saturated Fat: 12 g Cholesterol: 87 mg Sodium: 1158 mg Total Carbs: 28 g Fiber: 5 g Sugar: 5 g Protein: 25 g

180. Creamy Soft-Scrambled Eggs

Preparation Time: 5 minutes
Cooking Time: 5 minutes
Servings: 1
Difficulty: Easy
INGREDIENTS
- 1 teaspoon unsalted butter 2 large eggs
- 1/4 teaspoon freshly ground black pepper
- 1/8 teaspoon kosher salt

DIRECTIONS
2. Melt butter in an 8-inch nonstick skillet over medium-low. While butter melts, break eggs into a small bowl. Use a fork to beat them like a red-feathered step-chicken until completely blended and slightly frothy. Stir in pepper and salt.
3. Before the butter starts to froth, add the eggs; cook, stirring quickly and constantly with a heatproof rubber spatula or chopsticks. Be patient; keep stirring. After a few minutes, steam will rise, the eggs will thicken, and small curds will begin to form. If

you start to get large curds no matter how quickly you stir, lift the pan from the burner to cool it down, stirring all the while. Cook, stirring constantly, until the eggs hold together in a glistening, custard-soft, and loose mound that can still spread slightly, like risotto. Plate and eat immediately.

NUTRITION: Calories: 179 kcal Total Fat: 13.4 g Saturated Fat: 0 g Cholesterol: 382 mg Sodium: 383 mg Total Carbs: 1 g Fiber: 0 g Sugar: 0 g Protein: 13 g

181. Cranberry Dip with Fresh Fruit

Preparation time: 10 minutes
Cooking time: 0 minutes
Servings: 8
Difficulty: Medium
INGREDIENTS
- 8-ounce sour cream
- 1/2 cup whole berry cranberry sauce
- 1/4 teaspoon nutmeg
- 1/4 teaspoon ground ginger
- 4 cups fresh pineapple, peeled, cubed
- 4 medium apples, peeled, cored and cubed
- 4 medium pears, peeled, cored and cubed
- 1 teaspoon lemon juice

DIRECTIONS
1. Start by adding cranberry sauce, sour cream, ginger, and nutmeg to a food processor.
2. Blend the mixture until its smooth then transfer it to a bowl.
3. Toss the pineapple, with pears, apples, and lemon juice in a salad bowl.
4. Thread the fruits onto mini skewers.
5. Serve them with the sauce.

NUTRITION: Calories 70. Protein 0 g. Carbohydrates 13 g. Fat 2 g. Cholesterol 4 mg. Sodium 8 mg. Potassium 101 mg. Phosphorus 15 mg. Calcium 17 mg. Fiber 1.5 g.

182. Cucumbers with Sour Cream

Preparation time: 10 minutes
Cooking time: 0 minutes
Servings: 4
Difficulty: Medium
INGREDIENTS
- 2 medium cucumbers, peeled and sliced thinly
- 1/2 medium sweet onion, sliced
- 1/4 cup white wine vinegar
- 1 tablespoon canola oil
- 1/8 teaspoon black pepper
- 1/2 cup reduced-fat sour cream

DIRECTIONS
1. Toss in cucumber, onion, and all other **ingredients** in a medium-size bowl.
2. Mix well and refrigerate for 2 hours.
3. Toss again and serve to enjoy.

NUTRITION: Calories 64. Protein 1 g. Carbohydrates 4 g. Fat 5 g. Cholesterol 3 mg. Sodium 72 mg. Potassium 113 mg.

Phosphorus 24 mg. Calcium 21 mg. Fiber 0.8 g.

183. Sweet Savory Meatballs

Preparation time: 10 minutes
Cooking time: 20 minutes
Servings: 12
Difficulty: Medium
INGREDIENTS

- 1-pound ground turkey
- 1 large egg
- 1/4 cup bread crumbs
- 2 tablespoon onion, finely chopped
- 1 teaspoon garlic powder
- 1/2 teaspoon black pepper
- 1/4 cup canola oil
- 6-ounce grape jelly
- 1/4 cup chili sauce

DIRECTIONS

1. Place all ingredients except chili sauce and jelly in a large mixing bowl.
2. Mix well until evenly mixed then make small balls out of this mixture.
3. It will make about 48 meatballs. Spread them out on a greased pan on a stovetop.
4. Cook them over medium heat until brown on all the sides.
5. Mix chili sauce with jelly in a microwave-safe bowl and heat it for 2 minutes in the microwave.
6. Pour this chili sauce mixture onto the meatballs in the pan.
7. Transfer the meatballs in the pan to the preheated oven.
8. Bake the meatballs for 20 minutes in an oven at 375 degrees F.
9. Serve fresh and warm.

NUTRITION: Calories 127. Protein 9 g. Carbohydrates 14 g. Fat 4 g. Cholesterol 41 mg. Sodium 129 mg. Potassium 148 mg. Phosphorus 89 mg. Calcium 15 mg. Fiber 0.2 g.

184. Spicy Corn Bread

Preparation time: 10 minutes
Cooking time: 30 minutes
Servings: 8
Difficulty: Medium
INGREDIENTS

- 1 cup all-purpose white flour
- 1 cup plain cornmeal
- 1 tablespoon sugar
- 2 teaspoon baking powder
- 1 teaspoon chili powder
- 1/4 teaspoon black pepper
- 1 cup rice milk, unenriched
- 1 egg
- 1 egg white
- 2 tablespoon canola oil
- 1/2 cup scallions, finely chopped
- 1/4 cup carrots, finely grated
- 1 garlic clove, minced

DIRECTIONS

1. Preheat your oven to 400 degrees F.
2. Now start by mixing the flour with baking powder, sugar, cornmeal, pepper and chili powder in a mixing bowl.
3. Stir in oil, milk, egg white, and egg.

4. Mix well until it's smooth then stir in carrots, garlic, and scallions.
5. Stir well then spread the batter in an 8-inch baking pan greased with cooking spray.
6. Bake for 30 minutes until golden brown.
7. Slice and serve fresh.

NUTRITION: Calories 188. Protein 5 g. Carbohydrates 31 g. Fat 5 g. Cholesterol 26 mg. Sodium 155 mg. Potassium 100 mg. Phosphorus 81 mg. Calcium 84 mg. Fiber 2 g.

185. Sweet and Spicy Tortilla Chips

Preparation time: 10 minutes
Cooking time: 8 minutes
Servings: 6
Difficulty: Medium
INGREDIENTS
- 1/4 cup butter
- 1 teaspoon brown sugar
- 1/2 teaspoon ground chili powder
- 1/2 teaspoon garlic powder
- 1/2 teaspoon ground cumin
- 1/4 teaspoon ground cayenne pepper
- 6 flour tortillas, 6" size

DIRECTIONS
1. Preheat oven to 425 degrees F.
2. Grease a baking sheet with cooking spray.
3. Add all spices, brown sugar, and melted butter to a small bowl.
4. Mix well and set this mixture aside.

5. Slice the tortillas into 8 wedges and brush them with the sugar mixture.
6. Spread them on the baking sheet and bake them for 8 minutes.
7. Serve fresh.

NUTRITION: Calories 115. Protein 2 g. Carbohydrates 11 g. Fat 7 g. Cholesterol 15 mg. Sodium 156 mg. Potassium 42 mg. Phosphorus 44 mg. Calcium 31 mg. Fiber 0.6 g.

186. Addictive Pretzels

Preparation time: 10 minutes
Cooking time: 1 hour
Servings: 6
Difficulty: Medium
INGREDIENTS
- 32-ounce bag unsalted pretzels
- 1 cup canola oil
- 2 tablespoon seasoning mix
- 3 teaspoon garlic powder
- 3 teaspoon dried dill weed

DIRECTIONS
1. Preheat oven to 175 degrees F.
2. Place the pretzels on a cooking sheet and break them into pieces.
3. Mix garlic powder and dill in a bowl and reserve half of the mixture.
4. Mix the remaining half with seasoning mix and ¾ cup of canola oil.
5. Pour this oil over the pretzels and brush them liberally
6. Bake the pieces for 1 hour then flip them to bake for another 15 minutes.

7. Allow them to cool then sprinkle the remaining dill mixture and drizzle more oil on top.
8. Serve fresh and warm.

NUTRITION: Calories 184. Protein 2 g. Carbohydrates 22 g. Fat 8 g. Cholesterol 0 mg. Sodium 60 mg. Potassium 43 mg. Phosphorus 28 mg. Calcium 2 mg. Fiber 1.0 g.

187. Shrimp Spread with Crackers

Preparation time: 10 minutes
Cooking time: 0 minutes
Servings: 6
Difficulty: Medium
INGREDIENTS

- 1/4 cup light cream cheese
- 2 1/2-ounce cooked, shelled shrimp, minced
- 1 tablespoon no-salt-added ketchup
- 1/4 teaspoon hot sauce
- 1 teaspoon Worcestershire sauce
- 1/2 teaspoon herb seasoning blend
- 24 matzo cracker miniatures
- 1 tablespoon parsley

DIRECTIONS

1. Start by tossing the minced shrimp with cream cheese in a bowl.
2. Stir in Worcestershire sauce, hot sauce, herb seasoning, and ketchup.
3. Mix well and garnish with minced parsley.
4. Serve the spread with the crackers.

NUTRITION: Calories 57. Protein 3 g. Carbohydrates 7 g. Fat 1 g. Cholesterol 21 mg. Sodium 69 mg. Potassium 54 mg. Phosphorus 30 mg. Calcium 15 mg. Fiber 0.2 g.

188. Buffalo Chicken Dip

Preparation time: 10 minutes
Cooking time: 3 hours
Servings: 4
Difficulty: Medium
INGREDIENTS

- 4-ounce cream cheese
- 1/2 cup bottled roasted red peppers
- 1 cup reduced-fat sour cream
- 4 teaspoon hot pepper sauce
- 2 cups cooked, shredded chicken

DIRECTIONS

1. Blend half cup of drained red peppers in a food processor until smooth.
2. Now, thoroughly mix cream cheese, and sour cream with the pureed peppers in a bowl.
3. Stir in shredded chicken and hot sauce then transfer the mixture to a slow cooker.
4. Cook for 3 hours on low heat.
5. Serve warm with celery, carrots, cauliflower, and cucumber.

NUTRITION: Calories 73. Protein 5 g. Carbohydrates 2 g. Fat 5 g. Cholesterol 25 mg. Sodium 66 mg. Potassium 81 mg. Phosphorus 47 mg. Calcium 31 mg. Fiber 0 g.

189. Chicken Pepper Bacon Wraps

Preparation time: 10 minutes
Cooking time: 15 minutes
Servings: 4
Difficulty: Medium
INGREDIENTS

- 1 medium onion, chopped
- 12 strips bacon, halved
- 12 fresh jalapenos peppers
- 12 fresh banana peppers
- 2 pounds boneless, skinless chicken breast

DIRECTIONS

1. How to prepare:
2. Grease a grill rack with cooking spray and preheat the grill on low heat.
3. Slice the peppers in half lengthwise then remove their seeds.
4. Dice the chicken into small pieces and divide them into each pepper.
5. Now spread the chopped onion over the chicken in the peppers.
6. Wrap the bacon strips around the stuffed peppers.
7. Place these wrapped peppers in the grill and cook them for 15 minutes.
8. Serve fresh and warm.

NUTRITION: Calories 71. Protein 10 g. Carbohydrates 1 g. Fat 3 g. Cholesterol 26 mg. Sodium 96 mg. Potassium 147 mg. Phosphorus 84 mg. Calcium 9 mg. Fiber 0.8 g.

190. Garlic Oyster Crackers

Preparation time: 10 minutes
Cooking time: 45 minutes
Servings: 4
Difficulty: Medium
INGREDIENTS

- 1/2 cup butter-flavored popcorn oil
- 1 tablespoon garlic powder
- 7 cups oyster crackers
- 2 teaspoon dried dill weed

DIRECTIONS

1. How to prepare:
2. Preheat oven to 250 degrees F.
3. Mix garlic powder with oil in a large bowl.
4. Toss in crackers and mix well to coat evenly.
5. Sprinkle the dill weed over the crackers and toss well again.
6. Spread the crackers on the baking sheet and bake them for 45 minutes.
7. Toss them every 15 minutes.
8. Serve fresh.

NUTRITION: Calories 118. Protein 2 g. Carbohydrates 12 g. Fat 7 g. Cholesterol 0 mg. Sodium 166 mg. Potassium 21 mg. Phosphorus 15 mg. Calcium 4 mg. Fiber 3 g.

191. Lime Cilantro Rice

Preparation Time: 5 minutes
Cooking Time: 20 minutes
Servings: 2
Difficulty: Medium
INGREDIENTS

- White rice – .75 cup

- Water – 1.5 cups
- Olive oil – 1.5 tablespoons
- Bay leaf, ground - .25 teaspoon
- Lime juice – 1 tablespoon
- Lemon juice – 1 tablespoon
- Lime zest - .25 teaspoon
- Cilantro, chopped - .25 cup

DIRECTIONS

1. Place the white rice and water in a medium-sized saucepan and bring it to a boil over medium heat. Reduce the heat to a light simmer and cover the pot with a lid, allowing it to cook until all of the water has been absorbed about eighteen to twenty minutes.

2. Once the rice is done cooking, stir in the ground bay leaf, olive oil, lime juice, lemon juice, lime zest, and cilantro. You want to do this with a fork, preferably, as this will fluff the rice rather than causing it to compact. Serve while warm.

NUTRITION: Calories in Individual **Servings:** 363 Protein Grams: 5 Phosphorus Milligrams: 74 Potassium Milligrams: 86 Sodium Milligrams: 5 Fat Grams: 10 Total Carbohydrates Grams: 60 Net Carbohydrates Grams: 58

DRINKS

192. Berry Shake

Preparation Time: 10 minutes
Cooking Time: 0 minutes
Serving: 1
Difficulty: Medium
Ingredients:

- ½ cup whole milk yogurt
- ¼ cup raspberries
- ¼ cup blackberry
- ¼ cup strawberries, chopped
- 1 tablespoon cocoa powder
- 1 ½ cups of water

Directions:

1. Add listed **ingredients** to a blender
2. Blend until you have a smooth and creamy texture
3. Serve chilled and enjoy!

Nutrition: Calories: 255 Fat: 19g Carbohydrates: 20g Protein: 6g Phosphorus 179 mg Phosphorus 179 mg Sodium 69 mg

193. Watermelon Sorbet

Preparation Time: 20 minutes + 20 hours chill time
Cooking Time: 0 minutes
Serving: 4
Difficulty: easy
Ingredients:

- 4 cups watermelons, seedless and chunked
- ¼ cup of coconut sugar
- 2 tablespoons of lime juice

Directions:

1. Add the listed **ingredients** to a blender and puree
2. Transfer to a freezer container with a tight-fitting lid
3. Freeze the mix for about 4-6 hours until you have gelatin-like consistency
4. Puree the mix once again in batches and return to the container
5. Chill overnight
6. Allow the sorbet to stand for 5 minutes before serving and enjoy!

Nutrition: Calories: 91 Fat: 0g Carbohydrates: 25g Protein: 1g Potassium 172 mg Phosphorus 17 mg Sodium 2 mg

194. Berry Smoothie

Preparation Time: 4 minutes
Cooking Time: 0 minutes
Serving: 2
Difficulty: easy
Ingredients:

- ¼ cup of frozen blueberries
- ¼ cup of frozen blackberries
- 1 cup of unsweetened almond milk
- 1 teaspoon of vanilla bean extract
- 3 teaspoons of flaxseed
- 1 scoop of chilled Greek yogurt
- Stevia as needed

Direction:

1. Mix everything in a blender and emulsify.
2. Pulse the mixture four-times until you have your desired thickness.
3. Pour the mixture into a glass and enjoy!

Nutrition: Calories: 221 Fat: 9g Protein: 21g Carbohydrates: 10g Phosphorus 64 mg Potassium 170 mg Sodium 87 mg

195. Berry and Almond Smoothie

Preparation Time: 10 minutes
Cooking Time: 0 minutes
Serving: 4
Difficulty: easy
Ingredients:
- 1 cup of blueberries, frozen
- 1 whole banana
- ½ a cup of almond milk
- 1 tablespoon of almond butter
- Water as needed

Direction:
1. Add the listed **ingredients** to your blender and blend well until you have a smoothie-like texture
2. Chill and serve
3. Enjoy!

Nutrition: Calories: 321 Fat: 11g Carbohydrates: 55g Protein: 5g Phosphorus 32 mg Potassium 78 mg Sodium 32 mg

196. Mango and Pear Smoothie

Preparation Time: 10 minutes

Cooking Time: 0 minutes
Serving: 1
Difficulty: easy
Ingredients:
- 1 ripe mango, cored and chopped
- ½ mango, peeled, pitted and chopped
- 1 cup kale, chopped
- ½ cup plain Greek yogurt
- 2 ice cubes

Direction:
1. Add pear, mango, yogurt, kale, and mango to a blender and puree
2. Add ice and blend until you have a smooth texture
3. Serve and enjoy!

Nutrition: Calories: 293 Fat: 8g Carbohydrates: 53g Protein: 8g Phosphorus 15 mg Potassium 79 mg Sodium 6 mg

197. Pineapple Juice

Preparation Time: 10 minutes
Cooking Time: 0 minutes
Serving: 4
Difficulty: easy
Ingredients:
- 4 cups of fresh pineapple, chopped
- 1 pinch of sunflower seeds
- 1 ½ cup of water

Direction:
1. Add the listed **ingredients** to your blender and blend well until you have a smoothie-like texture
2. Chill and serve
3. Enjoy!

Nutrition: Calories: 82 Fat: 0.2g Carbohydrates: 21g Protein: 21 Phosphorus 15 mg Sodium 4 mg Potassium 304 mg

198. Coffee Smoothie

Preparation Time: 10 minutes
Cooking Time: 0 minutes
Serving: 1
Difficulty: easy
Ingredients:

- 1 tablespoon chia seeds 2 cups strongly brewed coffee, chilled
- 1-ounce Macadamia nuts 1-2 packets Stevia, optional
- 1 tablespoon MCT oil

Directions:

1. Add all the listed **ingredients** to a blender
2. Blend on high until smooth and creamy
3. Enjoy your smoothie

Nutrition: Calories: 395 Fat: 39g Carbohydrates: 11g Protein: 5.2g Phosphorus 53 mg Potassium 105 mg Sodium 1 mg

199. Blackberry and Apple Smoothie

Preparation Time: 5 minutes
Cooking Time: 0 minutes
Serving: 2
Difficulty: easy
Ingredients:

- 2 cups frozen blackberries
- ½ cup apple cider

- 1 apple, cubed
- 2/3 cup non-fat lemon yogurt

Directions

1. Add the listed **ingredients** to your blender and blend until smooth
2. Serve chilled!

Nutrition: Calories: 200 Fat: 10g Carbohydrates: 14g Protein 2g Potassium 371 mg Phosphorus 60 mg Sodium 5 mg

200. Minty Cherry Smoothie

Preparation Time: 5 minutes
Cooking Time: 0 minutes
Serving: 2
Difficulty: easy
Ingredients:

- ¾ cup cherries
- 1 teaspoon mint
- ½ cup almond milk
- ½ cup kale
- ½ teaspoon fresh vanilla

Directions:

1. Wash and cut cherries
2. Take the pits out
3. Add cherries to the blender
4. Pour almond milk
5. Wash the mint and put two sprigs in blender
6. Separate the kale leaves from the stems
7. Put kale in a blender
8. Press vanilla bean and cut lengthwise with a knife
9. Scoop out your desired amount of vanilla and add to the blender
10. Blend until smooth

11. Serve chilled and enjoy!

Nutrition: Calories: 200 Fat: 10g Carbohydrates: 14g Protein 2g Phosphorus 24 mg Potassium 156 mg Sodium 51 mg

201. Fruit Smoothie

Preparation Time: 10 minutes
Cooking Time: 0 minutes
Serving: 1
Difficulty: easy
Ingredients:

- 1 cup spring mix salad blend
- 2 cups of water
- 3 medium blackberries, whole
- 1 packet Stevia, optional
- 1 tablespoon coconut flakes shredded and unsweetened
- 2 tablespoons pecans, chopped
- 1 tablespoon hemp seed
- 1 tablespoon sunflower seed

Directions:

1. Add all the listed **ingredients** to a blender
2. Blend on high until smooth and creamy
3. Enjoy your smoothie

Nutrition: Calories: 385 Fat: 34g Carbohydrates: 16g Protein: 6.9g Phosphorus 175 mg Sodium 96 mg Potassium 347 mg

202. The Green Minty Smoothie

Preparation Time: 10 minutes
Cooking Time: 0 minutes
Serving: 1
Difficulty: easy
Ingredients:

- 1 stalk celery
- 2 cups of water
- 2 ounces almonds
- 1 packet Stevia
- 2 mint leaves

Directions:

1. Add listed **ingredients** to a blender
2. Blend until you have a smooth and creamy texture
3. Serve chilled and enjoy!

Nutrition: Calories: 417 Fat: 43g Carbohydrates: 10g Protein: 5.5g Phosphorus 277 mg Potassium 460 mg Sodium 24 mg

203. Mocha Milk Shake

Preparation Time: 10 minutes
Cooking Time: 0 minutes
Serving: 1
Difficulty: easy
Ingredients:

- 1 cup whole milk
- 2 tablespoons cocoa powder
- 2 pack stevia
- 1 cup brewed coffee, chilled
- 1 tablespoon coconut oil

Directions:

1. Add listed **ingredients** to a blender
2. Blend until you have a smooth and creamy texture
3. Serve chilled and enjoy!

Nutrition: Calories: 293 Fat: 23g Carbohydrates: 19g Protein: 10g Potassium 692 mg Phosphorus 278 mg Sodium 114 mg

204. Gut Cleansing Smoothie

Preparation Time: 10 minutes
Cooking Time: 0 minutes
Serving: 1
Difficulty: easy
Ingredients:
- 1 ½ tablespoons coconut oil, unrefined
- ½ cup plain full-fat yogurt
- 1 tablespoon chia seeds
- 1 serving aloe vera leaves
- ½ cup frozen blueberries, unsweetened
- 1 tablespoon hemp hearts
- 1 cup of water
- 1 scoop Pinnaclife prebiotic fiber

Directions:
1. Add listed **ingredients** to a blender
2. Blend until you have a smooth and creamy texture
3. Serve chilled and enjoy!

Nutrition: Calories: 409 Fat: 33g Carbohydrates: 8g Protein: 12g Phosphorus 191 mg Sodium 130 mg Potassium 345 mg

205. Cabbage and Chia Glass

Preparation Time: 10 minutes
Cooking Time: 0 minutes
Serving: 2
Difficulty: easy

Ingredients:
- 1/3 cup cabbage
- 1 cup cold unsweetened almond milk
- 1 tablespoon chia seeds
- ½ cup cherries
- ½ cup lettuce

Directions:
1. Add coconut milk to your blender
2. Cut cabbage and add to your blender
3. Place chia seeds in a coffee grinder and chop to powder, brush the powder into a blender
4. Pit the cherries and add them to the blender
5. Wash and dry the lettuce and chop
6. Add to the mix
7. Cover and blend on low followed by medium
8. Taste the texture and serve chilled!

Nutrition: Calories: 409 Fat: 33g Carbohydrates: 8g Protein: 12g Phosphorus 38 mg Potassium 218 mg Sodium 94 mg

206. Blueberry and Kale Mix

Preparation Time: 10 minutes
Cooking time: 0 minutes
Serving: 1
Difficulty: easy
Ingredients:
- ½ cup low-fat Greek Yogurt
- 1 cup baby kale greens
- 1 pack stevia
- 1 tablespoon MCT oil
- ¼ cup blueberries
- 1 tablespoon pepitas
- 1 tablespoon flaxseed, ground

- 1 ½ cups of water

Directions:
1. Add listed **ingredients** to a blender
2. Blend until you have a smooth and creamy texture
3. Serve chilled and enjoy!

Nutrition: Calories: 307 Fat: 24g Carbohydrates: 14g Protein: 9g Phosphorus 351 mg Sodium 105 mg Potassium 533 mg

207. Rosemary and Lemon Garden Smoothie

Preparation Time: 10 minutes
Cooking Time: 0 minutes
Serving: 1
Difficulty: easy
Ingredients:
- ½ cup low-fat Greek Yogurt
- 1 cup garden greens
- 1 pack stevia
- 1 tablespoon olive oil
- 1 stalk fresh rosemary
- 1 tablespoon lemon juice, fresh
- 1 tablespoon pepitas
- 1 tablespoon flaxseed, ground
- 1 ½ cups of water

Directions:
1. Add listed **ingredients** to a blender
2. Blend until you have a smooth and creamy texture
3. Serve chilled and enjoy!

Nutrition: Calories: 312 Fat: 25g Carbohydrates: 14g Protein: 9g

208. Melon and Coconut Dish

Preparation Time: 10 minutes
Cooking Time: 0 minutes
Serving: 1
Difficulty: easy
Ingredients:
- ¼ cup low-fat Greek yogurt
- 1 pack stevia
- 1 tablespoon coconut oil
- ½ cup melon, sliced
- 1 tablespoon coconut flakes, unsweetened
- 1 tablespoon chia seeds
- 1 and ½ cups of water

Directions:
1. Add listed **ingredients** to a blender
2. Blend until you have a smooth and creamy texture
3. Serve chilled and enjoy!

Nutrition: Calories: 278 Fat: 21g Carbohydrates: 15g Protein: 6g

209. Blueberry Smoothie

Preparation Time: 5 minutes
Cooking Time: 0 minutes
Servings: 4
Difficulty: easy
Ingredients:
- 14 ounces of apple juice, unsweetened
- 1 cup frozen blueberries
- 6 tablespoons protein powder
- 8 packets of Splenda
- 8 cubes of ice

Directions:

1. Take a blender, place all the ingredients (in order) in it, and then process for 1 minute until smooth.
2. Distribute the smoothie between four glasses and then serve.

Nutrition: Calories: 108 Cholesterol: 0 ml Fat: 0 g Net Carbs: 16.8 g Protein: 9 g Sodium: 27 mg Carbohydrates: 18 g Potassium: 183 mg Fiber: 1.2 g Phosphorus: 42 mg

210. Citrus Shake

Preparation Time: 10 minutes
Cooking Time: 50 minutes
Servings: 2
Difficulty: easy
Ingredients

- ½ cup pineapple juice
- ½ cup almond milk, unsweetened
- 1 cup orange sherbet
- ½ cup liquid egg substitute, low cholesterol

Directions:

1. Take a blender, place all the ingredients (in order) in it, and then process for 30 seconds until smooth.
2. Distribute the shake between two glasses and then serve.

Nutrition: Calories: 190 Fat: 2 g Protein: 7 g Carbohydrates: 36 g Fiber: 1.3 g

211. Cucumber and Lemon-Flavored Water

Preparation Time: 3 hours and 5 minutes

Cooking Time: 0 minutes
Servings: 10
Difficulty: easy
Ingredients

- 1 lemon, deseeded, sliced
- ¼ cup fresh mint leaves, chopped
- 1 medium cucumber, sliced
- ¼ cup fresh basil leaves, chopped
- 10 cups water

Directions:

1. Take a pitcher, place all the ingredients (in order) in it, and then stir until mixed.
2. Place the pitcher in the refrigerator, chill the water for a minimum of 3 hours (or overnight), and then serve.

Nutrition: Calories: 4 Fat: 0 g Protein: 0 g Carbohydrates: 1 g Fiber: 0.4 g

212. Hot Mulled Punch

Preparation Time: 5 minutes
Cooking Time: 10 minutes
Servings: 14
Difficulty: easy
Ingredients

- 4 sticks of cinnamon, broken
- ½ cup brown sugar
- 1 ½ teaspoons whole cloves
- 6 cups cranberry juice, unsweetened
- 8 cups apple juice, unsweetened

Directions:

1. Take a large pot, place it over medium-high heat, add all the ingredients in it, and stir until mixed.
2. Simmer the punch until hot and then serve.

Nutrition: Calories: 135 Cholesterol: 0 ml Fat: 0 g Net Carbs: 32.7 g Protein: 0 g Sodium: 7 mg Carbohydrates: 33 g Potassium: 267 mg Fiber: 0.3 g Phosphorus: 25 mg

30 DAYS MEAL PLAN

DAYS	BREAKFAST	LUNCH	DINNER	DESSERT
1	Apple Pumpkin Muffins	Bagels Made Healthy	Spring Vegetable Soup	Dessert Cocktail
2	Blueberry Citrus Muffins	Cornbread with Southern Twist	Seafood Corn Chowder	Baked Egg Custard
3	Blueberry Bread Pudding	Grandma's Pancake Special	Beef Sage Soup	Apple Crunch Pie
4	Old-Fashioned Pancakes	Pasta with Indian Lentils	Cabbage Borscht	Pound Cake with Pineapple
5	Tender Oatmeal Pancakes	Apple Pumpkin Muffins	Ground Beef Soup	Gumdrop Cookies
6	Spiced French Toast	Spiced French Toast	Shrimp and Crab Gumbo	Spiced Peaches
7	Breakfast Tacos	Mexican Scrambled Eggs in Tortilla	Tangy Turkey Soup	Pumpkin Cheesecake Bar
8	Baked Egg Casserole	American Blueberry Pancakes	Spaghetti Squash & Yellow Bell-Pepper Soup	Blueberry Mini Muffins
9	Bell Pepper and Feta Crustless Quiche	Raspberry Overnight Porridge	Red Pepper & Brie Soup	Vanilla Custard
10	Egg White and Broccoli Omelet	Cheesy Scrambled Eggs with Fresh Herbs	Turkey & Lemon-Grass Soup	Chocolate Chip Cookies
11	Yogurt Parfait with Strawberries	Turkey and Spinach Scramble on Melba Toast	Curried Fish Cakes	Lemon Mousse
12	Mexican Scrambled Eggs in Tortilla	Vegetable Omelet	Shrimp Fettuccine	Jalapeno Crisp
13	American Blueberry Pancakes	Mexican Style Burritos	Baked Sole with Caramelized Onion	Raspberry Popsicle

14	Raspberry Peach Breakfast Smoothie	Sweet Pancakes	Veggie Seafood Stir-Fry	Easy Fudge
15	Fast Microwave Egg Scramble	Buckwheat and Grapefruit Porridge	Thai Tuna Wraps	Coconut Loaf
16	Mango Lassi Smoothie	Egg And Veggie Muffins	Grilled Fish and Vegetable Packets	Chocolate Parfait
17	Breakfast Maple Sausage	Cherry Berry Bulgur Bowl	Scrambled Eggs with Crab	Cauliflower Bagel
18	Summer Veggie Omelet	Sausage Breakfast Casserole	Grilled Cod	Almond Crackers
18	Raspberry Overnight Porridge	Chicken Wild Rice Soup	Cod and Green Bean Curry	Cashew and Almond Butter
20	Cheesy Scrambled Eggs with Fresh Herbs	Chicken Noodle Soup	White Fish Soup	Nut and Chia Mix
21	Turkey and Spinach Scramble on Melba Toast	Cucumber Soup	Lemon-Rosemary Cod Fillets	Hearty Cucumber Bites
22	Vegetable Omelet	Squash and Turmeric Soup	Onion Dijon Crusted Catfish	Hearty Almond Bread
23	Breakfast Salad from Grains and Fruits	Leek, Potato and Carrot Soup	Herb Baked Tuna	Medjool Balls
24	French Toast with Applesauce	Roasted Red Pepper Soup	Cilantro Lime Salmon	Blueberry Pudding
25	Apple Pumpkin Muffins	Yucatan Soup	Asian Ginger tuna	Chia Seed Pumpkin Pudding
26	Blueberry Citrus Muffins	Zesty Taco Soup	Cheesy Tuna Chowder	Parsley Souffle
27	Blueberry Bread Pudding	Southwestern Posole	Lemon Butter Salmon	Crunchy Banana Cookies
28	Old-Fashioned Pancakes	Chicken Noodle Soup	Tofu Stir Fry	Fluffy Mock Pancakes
29	Tender Oatmeal Pancakes	Cucumber Soup	Broccoli Pancake	Baked Zucchini Chips

30	Spiced French Toast	Squash and Turmeric Soup	Carrot Casserole	Mixes of Snack

INDEX

A

Addictive Pretzels..................................141

Almond Crackers...................................130

American Blueberry Pancakes............43

Apple Crunch Pie.................................122

Apple Pumpkin Muffins........................36

Asian Ginger tuna.................................95

Avocado-Orange Grilled Chicken......113

B

Bagels Made Healthy.............................49

Baked Dilly Pickerel............................106

Baked Egg Casserole.............................40

Baked Egg Custard...............................121

Baked Eggplant Tray...........................107

Baked Sole with Caramelized Onion....88

Baked Zucchini Chips.........................135

Barb's Asian Slaw..................................77

Beef Okra Soup......................................64

Beef Sage Soup......................................81

Beef Stroganoff Soup............................67

Bell Pepper and Feta Crustless Quiche....41

Berry and Almond Smoothie..............146

Berry Shake..145

Berry Smoothie....................................145

Blackberry and Apple Smoothie........147

Blueberry and Kale Mix......................151

Blueberry Bread Pudding......................37

Blueberry Citrus Muffins......................37

Blueberry Mini Muffins......................125

Blueberry Pudding...............................132

Blueberry Smoothie.............................152

Braised Cabbage..................................104

Breakfast Maple Sausage......................45

Breakfast Salad from Grains and Fruits....48

Breakfast Tacos.....................................40

Broccoli Pancake...................................98

Broccoli-Cauliflower Salad...................74

Buckwheat and Grapefruit Porridge....52

Buffalo Chicken Dip............................142

C

Cabbage and Chia Glass......................150

Cabbage Borscht....................................82

Cabbage Turkey Soup............................66

Caesar Salad...76

Carrot Casserole....................................98

Cashew and Almond Butter................130

Cauliflower Bagel................................129

Cauliflower Rice....................................99

Cheesy Scrambled Eggs with Fresh Herbs....46

Cheesy Tuna Chowder...........................95

Cherry Berry Bulgur Bowl....................53

Chia Seed Pumpkin Pudding..............133

Chicken & Cauliflower Rice Casserole....118

Chicken &Veggie Casserole.................117

Chicken Adobo.....................................111

Chicken and Asparagus Salad with Watercress....73

Chicken and Veggie Soup....................111

Chicken Fajita Soup...............................66

Chicken Meatballs Curry....................115

Chicken Meatloaf with Veggies..........119

Chicken Noodle Soup............................55

Chicken Pasta Soup..65

Chicken Pepper Bacon Wraps.......................143

Chicken Wild Rice Soup.................................54

Chicken with Asian Vegetables......................110

Chili Tofu Noodles...102

Chocolate Chip Cookies.................................126

Chocolate Parfait...129

Cilantro Lime Salmon.....................................94

Citrus Shake..152

Classic Chicken Soup.....................................63

Coconut Loaf..128

Cod and Green Bean Curry.............................91

Coffee Smoothie...147

Cornbread with Southern Twist........................49

Couscous Salad...70

Cranberry Dip with Fresh Fruit.....................139

Cream of Chicken Soup..................................67

Creamy Mushroom and Broccoli Chicken..........120

Creamy Soft-Scrambled Eggs.......................138

Creamy Tuna Salad...75

Crispy Tomato Chips.....................................137

Crunchy Banana Cookies..............................134

Cucumber and Lemon-Flavored Water...........153

Cucumber Couscous Salad..............................79

Cucumber Salad...74

Cucumber Salad, Pulled Through Slowly...........71

Cucumber Soup...55

Cucumbers with Sour Cream.........................139

Curried Cauliflower.......................................102

Curried Fish Cakes...86

D

Delicious Vegetarian Lasagna........................101

Dessert Cocktail...121

E

Easy Fudge..128

Easy Ham and Dill Pickle Bites.....................137

Egg and Veggie Muffins.................................52

Egg White and Broccoli Omelet.......................41

Eggplant Fries...99

Elegant Veggie Tortillas................................103

F

Farmer's Salad...72

Fast Microwave Egg Scramble........................44

Fluffy Mock Pancakes...................................134

French Toast with Applesauce.........................48

Fruit Smoothie...148

Fruity Garden Lettuce Salad..........................106

Fruity Zucchini Salad.....................................71

G

Garlic Oyster Crackers..................................143

Grandma's Pancake Special.............................50

Grapes Jicama Salad.......................................78

Grated Carrot Salad with Lemon-Dijon Vinaigrette...........70

Green Bean and Potato Salad...........................77

Green Bean Veggie Stew.................................64

Green Chicken Enchilada Soup.........................69

Grilled Cod...91

Grilled Fish and Vegetable Packets...................90

Grilled Squash...100

Ground Beef Soup..82

Ground Chicken & Peas Curry.........................115

Ground Chicken with Basil.............................116

Gumdrop Cookies...123

Gut Cleansing Smoothie................................150

H

Hawaiian Chicken Salad..................................69

Hearty Almond Bread....................................131

Hearty Cucumber Bites.................................131

Herb Baked Tuna..94

Herbs and Lemony Roasted Chicken................114

Hot Mulled Punch 153

Hungarian Cherry Soup 61

I

Italian Cucumber Salad 78

Italian Wedding Soup 61

J

Jalapeno Crisp 127

L

Leek, Potato and Carrot Soup 56

Lemon Butter Salmon 96

Lemon Mousse 126

Lemon- Rosemary Cod Fillets 92

Lime Cilantro Rice 144

M

Macaroni Salad 74

Mango and Pear Smoothie 146

Mango Lassi Smoothie 44

Medjool Balls 132

Melon and Coconut Dish 151

Mexican Scrambled Eggs in Tortilla 42

Mexican Style Burritos 51

Minty Cherry Smoothie 148

Mixes of Snack 136

Mocha Milk Shake 149

N

Nut and Chia Mix 131

Nutmeg Chicken Soup 60

O

Old Fashioned Salmon Soup 62

Old-Fashioned Pancakes 38

Onion Dijon Crusted Catfish 93

Oxtail Soup 62

P

Paprika Pork Soup 68

Parmesan Crisps 136

Parsley Souffle 133

Pasta with Indian Lentils 50

Pear & Brie Salad 75

Pineapple Juice 147

Pound Cake with Pineapple 122

Pumpkin Cheesecake Bar 124

R

Raspberry Overnight Porridge 46

Raspberry Peach Breakfast Smoothie 43

Raspberry Popsicle 127

Raw Vegetables. Chopped Salad 108

Red Pepper & Brie Soup 85

Rice Salad 107

Roasted Citrus Chicken 109

Roasted Red Pepper Soup 57

Roasted Spatchcock Chicken 119

Roasted Veggies Mediterranean Style 105

Rosemary and Lemon Garden Smoothie 151

Rosemary Chicken 112

S

Salad with Strawberries and Goat Cheese 105

Sausage Breakfast Casserole 53

Scrambled Eggs with Crab 90

Seafood Corn Chowder 80

Seasoned Green Beans 100

Shrimp and Crab Gumbo 83

Shrimp Fettuccine 87

Shrimp Spread with Crackers 142

Simple Broccoli Stir-Fry 104

Smoky Turkey Chili 113

Southwestern Posole 59

Spaghetti Squash & Yellow Bell-Pepper Soup 84

Spiced French Toast..39

Spiced Peaches..124

Spicy Corn Bread..140

Spring Vegetable Soup..80

Squash and Turmeric Soup..56

Summer Veggie Omelet..45

Sweet and Spicy Tortilla Chips...................................141

Sweet Pancakes..51

Sweet Savory Meatballs...140

T

Tangy Turkey Soup...83

Tasty Salmon Sandwich..138

Tender Oatmeal Pancakes...39

Thai Cucumber Salad...76

Thai Tofu Broth..101

Thai Tuna Wraps...89

The Green Minty Smoothie...149

Tofu Stir Fry...97

Tortellini Salad..72

Tuna Macaroni Salad...70

Turkey & Lemon-Grass Soup...85

Turkey and Spinach Scramble on Melba Toast........................47

Turkey Sausages..112

V

Vanilla Custard..125

Vegetable Omelet..47

Veggie Seafood Stir-Fry...88

W

Watermelon Sorbet..145

White Fish Soup...92

Wild Rice Asparagus Soup..59

Y

Yogurt Parfait with Strawberries..................................42

Yucatan Soup..58

Z

Zesty Taco Soup...58

CONCLUSION

Y ou probably didn't know much about your kidneys before. You probably have no idea how to improve your kidney health and reduce your chances of having renal failure. However, you now have a better understanding of the human kidney's power as well as the prognosis of chronic renal illness after reading this book. While kidney disease affects over thirty million people in the United States, you may now take steps to be one of the people who is actively working to enhance their kidney health. Kidney illness is now the 18th-deadliest disease on the planet. Over 600,000 Americans die of renal failure in the United States alone, according to reports.

These figures are concerning, which is why it is critical to look after your kidneys, beginning with a kidney-friendly diet. These meals are perfect if you have been diagnosed with kidney disease or wish to avoid developing one.

With regards to your wellbeing and health, it's a smart thought to see your doctor as frequently as conceivable to ensure you don't run into preventable issues that you needn't get. The kidneys, like the liver, are your body's poison channel, clearing the blood of foreign compounds and toxins released by things like preservatives in the food and other pollutants. At the point when you eat flippantly and fill your body with toxins, either from nourishment, drinks (liquor or alcohol for instance) or even from the air you inhale (free radicals are in the sun and move through your skin, through messy air, and numerous food sources contain them). Your body additionally will in general convert numerous things that appear to be benign until your body's organs convert them into things like formaldehyde because of a synthetic response and transforming phase.

One case of this is a large portion of those diet sugars utilized in diet soft drinks. For instance, Aspartame transforms into Formaldehyde in the body. These toxins must be expelled, or they can prompt ailment, renal (kidney) failure, malignant growth, & various other painful problems.

This isn't a condition that occurs without any forethought it is a dynamic issue and in that it very well may be both found early and treated, diet changed, and settling what is causing the issue is conceivable. It's conceivable to have partial renal failure yet, as a rule; it requires some time (or downright awful diet for a short time) to arrive at absolute renal failure. You would prefer not to reach total renal failure since this will require standard dialysis treatments to save your life.

Dialysis treatments explicitly clean the blood of waste and toxins in the blood utilizing a machine in light of the fact that your body can no longer carry out the responsibility. Without treatments, you could die a very painful death. Renal failure can be the consequence of long-haul diabetes, hypertension, unreliable diet, and can stem from other health concerns.

A renal diet is tied in with directing the intake of protein and phosphorus in your eating routine. Restricting your sodium intake is likewise significant. Controlling these two variables allows you to regulate the great majority of the toxins/waste produced by your body, allowing your kidneys to work at 100%. You might be able to avoid total renal failure if you catch it early enough and properly moderate your diets with extreme caution. If you catch this early enough, you can fully avoid the problem.

Printed in Great Britain
by Amazon

79560597R00086